P9-CFM-689

PRAISE FOR *NO SAFE HARBOR*

"I can't think of anyone better qualified to tell cybersecurity war stories than Mark Sangster. This book is a riveting read, filled with details that people don't normally get to hear about."

DANNY BRADBURY, freelance writer and editor, contributing author to *Dark Reading*

"Mark Sangster provides a real wake-up call to law firms and companies of all sizes, especially for those that think they are too small or inconsequential to be the target of cybercrime. He draws from his expertise and experience to break down the misconceptions of cybersecurity and uses real-life examples to demonstrate the myriad ways cybercriminals can attack. Likening cyber-viruses to the unprecedented global pandemic, *No Safe Harbor* explains that cybersecurity has to become part of strategic planning; we can no longer just react to security issues—we have to have a mindset of protection."

STEVE SALKIN, managing editor, ALM's *Cybersecurity Law & Strategy*

"Mark Sangster has done an excellent job of turning 'war stories'— the campfire tales we share with each other at the bar—into an entertaining and informative book. If you're an executive concerned about protecting your organization from cybercrime, pick up this book; you don't need to be knowledgeable in cybersecurity to get something valuable out of it."

JON WASHBURN, chief information security officer (CISO), Stoel Rives LLP

"A great read about real-life cybersecurity incidents from the man who was there, playing cat and mouse with the hackers—I have seen Mark Sangster in action. His book gets to the root causes of why there is no safe harbor for any of us. Each chapter lists practical cybersecurity steps we should all take—starting today!"

MIKE STJOHN-GREEN, independent advisor, ex-GCHQ (retired)

"Mark Sangster's straightforward approach to storytelling and explaining by example helps clear the fog of cybersecurity to allow aspiring business leaders a better understanding of the risks, threats, and vulnerabilities faced by their companies in today's business environment—a world increasingly shaped of cybertheft, extortion, distraction, and destruction. Written in easy-to-understand language that anyone can grasp, and by analyzing the growing cybersecurity problem through the conceptual lens of businesspeople, Mark shares the successes and failures of others so that lessons can be learned and strategies and plans adjusted accordingly to avoid repeating the mistakes of recent history. *No Safe Harbor* is a must-read for any aspiring business leader."

RICHARD STAYNINGS, cybersecurity executive and thought leader; chief security strategist, Cylera; adjunct professor of cybersecurity risk management, The University of Denver, University College

"Mark Sangster brings to light the cyberattacks that never make the headlines. *No Safe Harbor* is a must-read for leaders developing tomorrow's technology. Mark reverse engineers the risks facing today's businesses to prevent our technical triumphs from becoming the cybercriminals' gain."

IAIN KLUGMAN, president and CEO, Communitech Corporation

"With the world experiencing an all-encompassing digital revolution that is reshaping seemingly every aspect of our business and personal lives, cybersecurity is more important than ever. *No Safe Harbor* is an engrossing journey into cybercrime that cleverly illustrates the chaos underneath the shiny façade of the modern internet."

MIRKO ZORZ, editor in chief, *Help Net Security*

"Manufacturers of all sizes are under constant threat from cybercriminals—yet most don't recognize that they are a target. Mark Sangster is a singularity in our sector, working tirelessly to rectify this dangerous misconception. He cuts through the technobabble and speaks directly to business leaders in their own language, providing them with clear tools and strategies they can use to protect their organizations and their supply chains."

CHRIS SCHMIDT, vice president of strategic partnerships,
National Association of Manufacturers (NAM)

"Mark Sangster's advice could not have arrived at a more propitious moment, as the work paradigm changes to remote information systems access as a default rather than an exception. *No Safe Harbor* reads like a collection of short stories, all revolving around a central theme: cybersecurity is a business risk and a people challenge; the approach to those people should be made, as Mark does so well, by appeals to common sense and should be documented in easy-to-understand frameworks. This book is essential reading for senior management and corporate directors."

KENNETH RASHBAUM, partner, Barton LLP

"Through frontline examples, Mark Sangster illuminates the fatal flaw in today's cyber-defense architecture—as long as business leaders and technical experts continue to speak at cross-purposes, efforts expended to get ahead of cybercriminals remain futile."

DAVE UNSWORTH, general partner, Information Venture Partners

"*No Safe Harbor* is a must-read for the twenty-first-century business professional. Cybercriminals' tactics have become increasingly sophisticated, and protecting a firm's digital assets is now every stakeholder's responsibility, not just IT's. In this book, Mark Sangster provides a concise, practical, and insightful guide into the motivations and practices of today's digital malefactors. The stories he shares are true, and will open the reader's eyes as to what to expect. Cyber-threats are real, and this book offers solid advice on how to protect your company while remaining competitive."

JOSEPH T. LYNN, legal technology expert and thought leader

"As the practice of law grows evermore multifaceted and interdisciplinary, educating the legal profession about the opportunities, challenges, and nuances of technology becomes increasingly crucial. Through vivid and engaging anecdotes and sharp insights into the realities of professional practice, Mark Sangster's *No Safe Harbor* makes cybersecurity accessible and engaging, and provides valuable perspectives for lawyers at all stages of their careers."

ROBERT MAHARI, president, Harvard Law and Technology Society

"Cybersecurity budgets have never been higher, so why do major brands with deep pockets continue to regularly experience major breaches that shut down their operations, while the impact of cybercrime on the global economy grows north of 1 percent of GDP per annum? In a world with an increasing use of rhetoric around absolutes and finger-pointing, *No Safe Harbor* offers a unique and refreshing insight into the multidimensional nature of modern cybersecurity with a foundational thesis that a culture of risk mitigation and continuous improvement are central to defensive strategies. Blending real-world examples with practical guidance, this book is highly relevant to executives and business leaders."

ALEX JINIVIZIAN, vice president of strategy and international marketing, eSentire

NO SAFE HARBOR

THE INSIDE TRUTH ABOUT CYBERCRIME— AND HOW TO PROTECT YOUR BUSINESS

MARK SANGSTER

NO SAFE HARBOR

PAGE TWO BOOKS

Copyright © 2020 by Mark Sangster

All rights reserved. No part of this book may be
reproduced, stored in a retrieval system or transmitted, in any form or by any
means, without the prior written consent of the publisher or a license from
The Canadian Copyright Licensing Agency (Access Copyright). For a copyright
license, visit www.accesscopyright.ca or call toll free to 1-800-893-5777.

Some names and identifying details have been changed to
protect the privacy of individuals and organizations.

The views expressed herein are those of the author and do not necessarily
reflect the official policy or position of any other agency, organization, employer,
or company. The material and information contained in this publication is
for general information purposes only. You should not rely upon the material
or information in this publication as a basis for making any business, legal, or
any other decisions. While the author endeavors to keep the information up
to date and correct, the author makes no representations or warranties of any
kind, express or implied, about the completeness, accuracy, reliability, suitabil-
ity, or availability with respect to this publication or the information, products,
services, or related graphics contained in the publication for any purpose. Any
reliance you place on such material is therefore strictly at your own risk.

Cataloguing in publication information is
available from Library and Archives Canada.
ISBN 978-1-989603-42-0 (hardcover)
ISBN 978-1-989603-43-7 (ebook)

Page Two
www.pagetwo.com

Edited by James Harbeck
Copyedited by Kendra Ward
Proofread by Alison Strobel
Jacket design by Peter Cocking and Fiona Lee
Interior design by Fiona Lee
Printed and bound in Canada by Friesens
Distributed in Canada by Raincoast Books
Distributed in the US and internationally
by Publishers Group West, a division of Ingram

20 21 22 23 24   5 4 3 2 1

mbsangster.com

For my three angels.

Together, we will make sure that

color never goes out of our life.

CONTENTS

INTRODUCTION

I **WAS STANDING IN** the boardroom of a prominent law firm, listening to a heated discussion between a security executive and a managing partner. I was leaning back, patiently observing their brackish conversation about suspending the network credentials of a compromised account belonging to a rainmaker. The best practices of the security executive conflicted with the concerns of the seasoned lawyer, who was worried about how this logical action might tarnish a rising star in the firm.

We were in the middle of conducting a cyber data breach simulation. It was designed to intentionally clash security best practice with business realities and make them face their own version of the "Kobayashi Maru"—the fictitious no-win training simulation from the *Star Trek* universe.

We hadn't even got to the hard stuff yet.

I had arranged a scenario based on facts I had cobbled together from real-life events. There wasn't one right answer, but there were a lot of details to consider, some that had never occurred to either of them. They were forced to connect, criticize, and ultimately collaborate on what should happen next.

And that's the point.

IT practices and business reason are going to collide in these situations. These two professionals, equals in their own subject matter, were learning firsthand that, as I told them at the start, security isn't an IT issue to fix, it's a business risk to manage.

And that's a hard lesson to learn.

Most business leaders find out the hard way.

Let's take an example of when IT staff proactively protected one of the largest law firms, DLA Piper, but unintentionally exposed the firm's cyber outage to the public. An employee posted a sign in the lobby of the law firm's office in Sydney that read, "All network services are down, do not turn on your computers! Please remove all laptops from docking stations and keep turned off. No exceptions." A visitor snapped a picture and posted it on a social media outlet, and a hawkeyed journalist caught the post and turned it into a headline, suggesting that the firm's sensitive information on its corporate and private clients hadn't remained confidential. While a breach in the firm's payroll software was revealed to be the cause of the leak, and DLA Piper had the FBI and other international agencies on the case, the company's reputation took an immediate hit.

It sounds ridiculous, but that's all it takes.

It was a wake-up call for the industry. Until then, most law firms considered data breaches the domain of major banks and Fortune 500 companies. As famous bank robber Willie Sutton reputedly told a reporter on his arrest, criminals rob banks "because that's where the money is"[1]—not law firms filled with paper and books. And it's a reasonable assumption, given that most headlines cover large-scale breaches and rarely expose the ones that occur in smaller businesses. But it's smaller and midsized firms that take the brunt of cyberattacks, suffering massive financial losses, costly operational disruptions, and even irreversible damage to their reputations.[2]

Not only law firms labor under this misconception. Most companies do. Hospitals and clinics, manufacturing organizations, accounting and marketing firms, educational institutions, and so on. As Sutton's law says, one should first consider the obvious. Or, as a medical school professor would say, "When you hear hooves, think horses, not zebras."[3]

Company leaders think: "We are a little business in a Midwest town. We are too small for anyone to target us. We don't have anything worth stealing. How would some criminal in Russia or North Korea even know we exist?" But cybercriminals don't discriminate by employee count or EBITDA-positive financial statements. And through a long process of socialization, they've learned who pays ransoms, who has access to money, and who has data worth stealing for resale on dark markets.

If you don't think you're a target, you're not going to do enough to protect your business, and you'll leave yourself exposed to digital horse thieves.

Over the last five years, I've watched the volume of attacks increase and the tools and tactics of cybercriminals evolve and improve faster than the security industry can respond. I've seen too many good companies and good people fall victim to criminal adversaries. And it seemed that many of these attacks could have been prevented, or at least minimized. The same factors created a common patchwork connecting these events. It was like each company was repeating the same cycle of false assumptions, check-box mentality towards cybersecurity, and a constant flow of damaging and expensive data breaches.

Worst of all, these companies were all suffering in silence, breaking a valuable chain required to provide vicarious learning and improvement. These companies were lining up outside the kitchen to be escorted in, one at a time, to touch the stove so they would learn it was hot and not touch it again.

And in the midst of that conversation with the security executive and a managing partner, I knew I could keep running these security event simulations in boardroom after boardroom, like I'd done at more than a hundred organizations and for thousands of attendees, or I could do what the headlines had failed to do.

I could tell their stories.

My goal is not to point fingers or cast blame, but to expose the fundamental causes of cybercrime, to offer new ways of looking at the problem, and to start a conversation to help these organizations protect themselves from the next cyberattack.

Throughout the book, I explore multiple security stories for the unique lessons we can learn. In some cases, I have renamed or in other ways anonymized these entities. My job is, after all, to keep them out of the headlines. In other cases, where I have named organizations, it is because the stories are publicly available. It's important to remember, I am in no way implying these organizations were negligent or failed in the duties in some way. People do the best they can in the heat of the moment. They make difficult and potentially costly decisions in uncertain conditions and with limited information. The military has an apt expression for this: VUCA. It stands for volatile, uncertain, complex, and ambiguous.

You are also going to read about stories beyond the data breach headlines. You will read about air crashes, oil drilling disasters, and architectural failures. Although they seem unrelated, they draw parallels that offer critical insights we often cannot see from our vantage point, nose deep in the mire of cyber budgets, resource constraints, and press and peers lining up to find a scapegoat.

The purpose of this book is to ask *what* is responsible, not *who* is to blame. It's about changing the narrative from point-and-blame to seeking 360-degree accountability and continuous improvement.

In this book, we'll clarify the risks and prioritize your objectives, and I'll provide clear guidance for small to midsized businesses to build a right-sized cybersecurity program that will protect what matters. We'll look at anecdotes about all of these risks to demystify the problems and that you can use to assemble your own security program and demonstrate its value to your leadership team.

1

CHAOS REIGNS

WHAT YOU DON'T know might not kill you, but it could destroy you. And sometimes destruction comes in forms that we can't anticipate.

Like teddy bears.

On the surface, the 2017 CloudPets hack sounds like a joke. Spiral Toys, the inventor of CloudPets, created the bears, unicorns, and other fluffy stuffed animals to send and receive voice messages between children and their parents. Like Genesis Toys's My Friend Cayla doll and i-Que Intelligent Robot, Mattel's Hello Barbie doll, Hasbro's Furby Connect, and Toy-fi Teddy, all of which operate using possibly unstable Bluetooth connections, CloudPets were the object of a bombardment of requests to parents over Christmas 2016, and they flooded homes and schools as fast as they could be churned out of factories. But when CloudPets became involved in a data breach of more than 800,000 user accounts, hackers not only got the email and password data that were used to link the toys to users' app accounts, they could ostensibly begin to control those voice recordings. The breach began to resemble a cut-rate horror film more than a simple hack, despite the fact that the company wrote off security experts' concerns.[1] Even though it never went this far, it was technically possible for these toys to share insidious messages with children the world over, like a mass-produced set of Wi-Fi-enabled Chucky dolls. By 2020, well after the company went under, the CloudPets case was still being unraveled because thousands of the toys were still for resale on eBay, among other sites, despite a commitment from the retailer to pull the line.

Of course teddy bears may be the least of our concerns about cybersecurity, but the lack of forethought in this case shows exactly why our technological choices can lead to the fatal destruction of educational institutions, business organizations, law enforcement agencies, hospitals, and local and state governments, in addition to individuals.

A cybercrime happens every thirty-nine seconds, but the fact is that many digital criminals are patient, waiting until they collect the right combination of data before selling it to someone who will use it for nefarious purposes.[2] As you read these words, hackers and data brokers are also auctioning off customer information stolen from thousands of bait-and-switch websites, where people enter their personal identifiable information to get a Walmart gift card, download privileged access to an elite event from a high-value credit card, or check the progress of a world pandemic. In the first six months of 2019, 4.1 billion online records were accessed.[3] American consumer data, including driving and arrest records, genealogy reports, and even everyday phone number search patterns are being codified, organized, and packed up for the world's highest bidders. Not to mention that, in the better part of ten years, we've moved almost all of our mundane tasks onto the internet. We order our marriage certificates online. We check out books from virtual libraries. We take university courses and we post pictures of our dogs and grandmothers online. In fact, people would rather lose their wallet than their smartphone—the latter carries more value and critical information. Every single thing we do is online, and breaches are increasing because the devices we use are mobile and easier to infiltrate.

And all of it, all of that data, everything we type into our browsers, is for sale. Or for rent. The FBI reports that cyber-criminal networks will, for a fee, lend out a hacker to find data on a specific person, essentially selling access to the networks of victims around the world. It's personal espionage at large. That may be why Pew Research Center says that in 2018, 64 percent of Americans had incurred a serious breach of their data, and the FBI's Internet Crime Complaint Center (IC3) has recently revealed that web-based crime, over the course of the last calendar year on record, came with an almost $3 billion price tag.[4] Data collected by the National Security Agency in 2017 revealed that only 11 percent of U.S. companies had not experienced any fraudulent occurrence on their ecommerce sites in the past year,[5] which shows how large the problem is, and how it continues to affect the economic security of businesses as well as of individuals, which therefore constitutes a threat to the economic system of the country on a broad scale, and therefore affects the international economic system as well. Stories of massive data breaches pervade headlines, littered with a who's who of major brand names of banks and retailers.

And while glaring, these stories are only the tip of the iceberg. The big names garner the lion's share of coverage and little spotlight is left to illuminate the enormous volume of smaller businesses that are plagued by cyberattacks, just like their larger-enterprise cousins. This lack of coverage propagates a false sense of security in the belief that their small size makes them undetectable to hackers, or that their seemingly innocuous business activities are of little interest to criminal syndicates based on the other side of the globe. The reality is that smaller businesses such as financial investment brokers, law and accounting organizations, hospitals and health care clinics, and manufacturers around the globe, as well as individual people, are daily victims of cybercrime. And smaller organizations labor under the adage that people rob banks because that's where the money is. But there is money in the valuable information managed by these businesses. Although their size is small, the volume of such businesses adds up to losses in the billions every year.

At the same time, our definition of computer crime of any sort is problematic because it is connected to a loose set of frauds or abuses in which computerized data or software play a major role, but which continue to change. It can include theft, economic espionage, financial fraud, embezzlement, invasion of privacy, and trespassing.

Why, exactly, is this happening right now? On a superficial level, cybercrime happens because our world is becoming more dependent on the internet, and more economically complex at the same time. Because of the expansion of online communication and commerce, computer crime is linked to criminal activities such as intimidation, theft, extortion, fraud, or money laundering on a broad scale. This is often not something that takes place in a single location but is instead organized on a global basis, with a range of international actors who are connected to one another through dark channels that are difficult to locate by those working in criminal justice. These are threats not only to individuals and companies but also to national security, as they have the ability to take down components of our critical infrastructure that could devastatingly affect the health, safety, and well-being of millions of innocent people.

But there's a deeper story underneath this surface, and one that has to do with the increasing chaos that's affecting our collective, newly globalized experience.

The chaos revolution

One sleepless night, I turned on a BBC documentary on fractal science and chaos theory by Jim Al-Khalili, a British theoretical physicist.[6] A fractal is a complex pattern that repeats itself infinitely as you zoom out or in on it. You've probably seen fractal images on your computer screensaver at some point, with thousands of colors twisting away from you. Chaos theory, on the other hand, looks at unpredictable results that can come from the interaction of complex factors. Think of the butterfly effect, with a ripple that starts somewhere and increases in intensity and changes direction as it moves throughout space and time, bombarded by countless tiny forces within its immediate vicinity. Fractals interact with chaos in that, when we repeat patterns endlessly, they don't stay the same. It's a little like looking back and forth between two mirrors: these repeating reflections represent us but also deviate as they move and shift through the glass. The documentary, as it unfolded, revealed something very interesting about who we are as a species: no matter how much we try to control things, our daily lives are very much at the mercy of increasingly unpredicted outcomes, infinitely complex and twisting in different directions than we expected.

That's exactly what's happening right now in our economy.

The Industrial Revolution began between 150 and two hundred years ago, depending on who you ask. It made it possible for us to increase our technology at an ever-more-rapid pace. In this time period, there was a push towards the construction of efficient processes by which to create ideal economic, social, and scientific outcomes to ensure the best possible human experience. This push towards perfection, scientists thought, meant that if we were able to create something once, we could also use science to make it better, faster, easier, and cheaper. The most deleterious forms of labor could be replaced with technologies that would improve the quality of life for those in the poorest sectors of our society. Now, as in the nineteenth century, we are currently experiencing declining costs, increasing productivity, and reduced excess capacity in the form of too many goods, which has necessitated companies' downsizing and even their exit.

In Lewis Carroll's *Through the Looking-Glass*, the Red Queen says, about her own queendom, "Now, here, you see, it takes all the running you can do, to keep in the same place." Drawn from biology theory, the Red Queen Effect tells us exactly why we're in this state at the current time. This hypothesis proposes that, like biological organisms in an ecosystem, we must constantly adapt in order to survive, and, when that happens, we find ourselves in security dilemmas.[7] Think about the cold war arms race and the rapidly increasing perceived need to one-up our enemies with security tactics that ended up in the mass creation of nuclear weapons, ironically named MAD: mutually assured destruction. Each side, without having all the needed information, simply decides to outpace the other to gain an invisible advantage. Both sides keep going because they can't find a reasonable place to stop without feeling as if they're putting themselves in jeopardy.

The same goes for technology. We've switched our focus towards data. We've discovered that the product of the future is not something we build and sell to the consumer, it *is* the consumer. Technology helps us obtain more information, more quickly, driving better, faster, easier, and cheaper ways to mine it.

When the consumer becomes the product, those increasingly unpredicted outcomes change. The chaos is no longer only about where to find and exploit natural resources or capital. The chaos is all about us: our identities, our privacy, our governance systems. And, all too often, unchecked unintended consequences. We're getting really good at the kind of one-upmanship that marked the cold war, except we're talking in binary code rather than on red phones that connected the Oval Office to the Kremlin.

Hacking isn't a basement-dwelling-loser game anymore. It's a business just like any other. Whether we're talking about smash-and-grab online robberies or sophisticated takedowns, many of those doling out the attacks are backed by organized crime, nation-states, and money moguls. And sure, they're leveling our systems from as far away as Russia and China, but big-time cybercriminals also operate right in our backyards.

Cybercrime: a growth industry

Cybercrime will only continue to grow. And it will grow in ferocity and frequency. Consider the law enforcement lenses of means, motives, and opportunity. The means in terms of proven malware and techniques are readily available at a reasonable price and simply require gaming-level tech skills. The motives are obvious: cybercrime is lucrative and estimated to cost the world $6 trillion by 2021—that's double that of the losses five years ago.[8] In terms of opportunity, most criminals are beyond the reach of the law and operate with impunity. They work in lawless, politically destabilized countries, or are on the payroll of these corrupt regimes. In the United States and United Kingdom, the arrest and conviction rates for cybercrimes are less than 1 percent, and they are often tried in absentia.[9]

This makes cybercrime a very alluring prospect for solo actors, organized crime cartels, and nation-states alike. Think of it like this: To rob a bank, you need a cool mask to hide your identity, and firearms so the bank employees and patrons take you seriously. In the robbery, you are likely to get shot by security or first responders. And the odds are, you will go to jail for your transgression. With cybercrime, you use simple and readily available tools to attack a bunch of faceless people on the other side of the world to make a quick $500 or $50,000 defrauding them. And you're never going to be arrested, let alone be convicted and serve time.

It's not an issue of immorality, but rather one of survival. Imagine trying to feed your family on a pittance by driving a cab in some third world country, or you make a quick buck with your mobile phone or laptop. It's simple economics. Cybercrime is here to stay. In a digital world, crime appears virtual but we suffer the real-world consequences. In fact, we witnessed this self-preservation mechanism in full force during the COVID-19 outbreak as people hoarded toilet paper and hand sanitizer. It's every person for themselves in times of chaos.

One of the problems with this situation is that there is no single governance practice, legal accord, or set of technological tools in cybersecurity that continuously improve outcomes for businesses or individuals: we're all on our own. As the breadth and depth of online interactions increase, the criminal justice system has been forced to not only keep up but also to predict what can be done to reduce the possibility of these crimes before they take place. But the Department of Justice's role is often made harder by the extent to which citizens give access permissions to third-party organizations. Every time we click "I Agree," we're giving away our rights.

The current law framework is moving towards a system where, instead of placing the onus on the criminal justice system to deter crime through punishment, policies are created to dry up the demand for data in the first place, which places an extra legal burden on companies to control the way in which they create, use, and sell data that is linked to customer accounts. Companies sanctioned under this new framework will be largely cut out of the international financial system and be prevented from owning property in the United States and its international partners in the law. At the same time, other legal pundits suggest that this approach may not be feasible because of the extent to which it is necessary for laws to be developed to control the rise of hackers.[10] But companies cannot create the framework to prosecute crimes, and the law isn't fast enough to cull the herd of hackers out there right now.

That's why businesses should care more about defending their virtual gates that keep out the invisible chaos of the online world.

The wolves at the gate

The cyber risk equation includes some variables that can be quantified. Most threat profiles are based on the industry and geography in which the organization operates. Banks, hospitals, law firms, manufacturing, and education institutions top the list.

Many of these industries are governed either directly or indirectly by regulatory agencies that dictate minimum standards of operations. Unfortunately, many organizations believe that compliance to these standards means they are secure. And that's patently false. Emerging technology like cloud-based services and Internet of Things (IoT) introduce unknowns, cause confusion or misunderstanding around shared security responsibilities, and provide new avenues through which criminals can exploit an organization.

But the greatest variable is the one most businesses can control: culture. Properly aligning security objectives to business goals and risk tolerances means creating an equilibrium. It means budgets and resourcing track back to risk assessments. It's where companies can convert ones and zeros into dollar signs.

Companies think in terms of lost revenue, fines or penalties, and cleanup costs. And they can be whopping. For example, when Norsk Hydro, a massive aluminum manufacturer with thirty thousand employees across forty countries, was hit by a devastating ransomware attack, the price tag was somewhere around $52 million.[11]

But dollar signs are sometimes camouflaged or deferred in the intangible consequences of a material cyber breach. Sometimes, the biggest cost is to the organization's reputation. And reputation is not something an organization can insure nor spend money to reform.

Mossack Fonseca, the Panamanian law firm at the center of the Panama Papers scandal, shuttered its operations citing irrecoverable reputational damage resulting from its role in systemic offshore tax sheltering. In a statement, the firm blamed "reputational deterioration" and a "media campaign" that "have occasioned an irreversible damage that necessitates the obligatory ceasing of public operations."[12]

When we talk about hackers, who are we talking about, exactly? We're inclined to think about the kinds of cybercrimes that happened in the past, and those who committed them, rather than what's happening right now. Those guys coding in their mom's basement, trying to break into corporate sites for fun? We call them script kiddies, and while they're still out there, they're the least of our worries. The same goes for smash-and-grab criminals like those "Nigerian princes," ones who conduct opportunist crimes by sending out emails to catch the least-informed people, or trying to phish for money during a crisis like Hurricane Katrina, the Australian bush fires, or the COVID-19 pandemic. They're also not typically on our radar because they come and go, and most people have heard of their scams. Hacktivists still exist as well—Anonymous comes to mind—but they're not as much of a risk or influence as they once were, and their actions often result in digital protest rather than criminal damage.

What we do have to worry about are the real criminals in our cybersphere: organized crime syndicates. These are highly aggressive, global, and large scale. And they don't often get caught. Our global law enforcement capacity has not yet come to terms with the huge network of attackers that are spread out in locations all over the world, and who communicate with each other through hidden means.[13] The problem is, of course, that even if the U.S. government identifies a hacker and brings charges, that individual may be out of reach of local courts, which means that most cases tend to be civil rather than criminal, and they take years to play out.[14]

On top of this, organized crime syndicates aren't just businesses, they're linked to and often incorporated into government activities. Nation-states such as China, North Korea, and Russia, and many more, employ hackers to not only commit espionage directly but also to hobble corporate entities in different countries in order to get at the data they need.

And let's not forget about corporate ecosystems themselves. Who are your partners, contractors, consultants, vendors? Who works for your company? Could a trusted colleague turn out to be a malicious insider or, at the very least, someone who gets duped and is an unwilling participant in a cybercrime?

How can you protect your company, knowing all of these wolves are at your gate?

Regardless of size, all businesses have big-company problems. And the government agencies, regulators, law enforcement arms, and standards councils tend to build security mechanisms aimed at large enterprise where resources are far more abundant, in-house expertise is more likely, and budgets flow from larger reserves. This leaves the majority of businesses confounded by the daunting task of tackling big business cybersecurity, with a fraction of the budget, time, and experts to make a successful go. It's a monumental task. How does one boil the ocean?

Learning cybersecurity is just like becoming an elite boxer. If you build muscle memory through training, your brain will protect you when you face down an opponent in real life and fear and panic threaten to overwhelm you. You'll know where to land the first and the last punch.

This book is about finding, practicing, and using your muscle memory for risk management and cybersecurity. It's my aim to make sure that you'll know exactly what to do so that you can prevent getting hit, as much as it is possible to block those punches.

When you do get hit, and there is every chance that you will, you won't go down without a fair fight.

2

NO MORE ONES
AND ZEROS

IN THE WEEK before Hurricane Ella was expected to reach
New York City in 1978, police quietly monitored ten blocks
of Manhattan at 53rd Street and Lexington Avenue as they
had been doing for the past month. Over 2,500 Red Cross vol-
unteers were waiting at the ready. While people walked by the
corner of the building that stood there, hundreds of welders
were taking panels off the inside walls and reinforcing them
with steel plates one by one, no one the wiser. The New York
City newspaper strike taking place meant that everything could
be kept quiet and that the meticulous and time-consuming
work was never revealed to the outside world, at the time.

The brand-new Citicorp tower, the seventh-tallest building
in the world then, wasn't going to fall down.

A few years earlier, structural engineer William LeMessurier was sitting at a table, absentmindedly looking at a plate
of Greek food, when he had an idea about how he could solve
a problem he'd been toying with for weeks. St. Peter's Lutheran
Church was in the way of the planned skyscraper. It was an

old, ramshackle Victorian-era building that had occupied one of the busiest corners of the city since it had been known as New Amsterdam, and St. Peter's had sold the lot to Citicorp under the expectation that they would be able to retain space for, and then pay to build, a new, modern church to be accommodated on the same block. LeMessurier thought that the idea was ridiculous, but it was a reality that he had to live with. All of a sudden, it came to him: create a building that could be cantilevered above the block, with room for the church on the underside. Long connected to the architect Hugh Stubbins, Jr., and a part-time professor at Harvard University, LeMessurier knew that his team would be up for the challenge as he rapidly mapped out his ideas on a napkin. He imagined the building on stilts, but to achieve that goal he also had to build an exceptionally light structure that could withstand wear and tear, the long-term settling of the building materials, and weather.

Fast-forward a few months and LeMessurier and Stubbins had put together a plan for a fifty-nine-story tower on the same stilts imagined on that spare napkin. The biggest question, from an engineering point of view, was how to deal with the winds that blew into the city off the Atlantic coast every autumn. Engineers knew that perpendicular winds, those that struck the building on each face, were the biggest threat. LeMessurier had accounted for them. He meticulously calculated the equations that would ensure that the tower could withstand gale forces, including those that could result from hurricanes, and not only added a tuned mass damper to stabilize the building but also created an infrastructure with a unique chevron design, rather than typical steel girders in rows and columns, so that nothing could touch it.

So confident was LeMessurier about the building's unique strength that he began to boast about it in his Harvard lectures, extolling his own vision and ingenuity about the chevron design. He even believed that his structural genius ought to have been a feature of the architecture, rather than lying hidden behind the tower's glass panels. In a 1995 interview on the Citicorp tower he admitted to *New Yorker* reporter Joe Morgenstern, "I'm very vain. I would have liked my stuff to be expressed on the outside of the building, but Stubbins wouldn't have it. In the end, I told myself I didn't give a damn— the structure was there, it'd be seen by God."[1]

But on one of those afternoons at Harvard University, a student working on her undergraduate thesis picked up on something that LeMessurier ought to have taken into consideration. It wasn't just the perpendicular winds that had to be factored in: there were also quartering winds. The structural engineer had forgotten all about the winds that strike a building at its corners, ones that could shatter the tensile strength of a building created on stilts, especially under the right conditions. Diane Hartley, the student, wrote a paper read by one of LeMessurier's teaching and engineering assistants arguing that it would be possible for a hurricane force windstorm to take out the building entirely, and because of its size, level New York City for several blocks.

Hartley never met LeMessurier, but her work did end up landing on his desk after she pressured the assistant to take her calculations seriously. Quartering winds would increase the tension on the building by a whopping 40 percent, leading to a critical failure of every bolt on the chevron structure. It was a potentially disastrous design flaw, not only for the engineer and architect, but also for the company that hired them, and for the city that allowed the plans to be actualized, and for the people who worked and lived in the vicinity.

A toppling Citicorp tower would act like the first domino to fall in a long line of dominoes, potentially toppling multiple buildings or crushing its smaller neighbors.

For a man with a God complex, LeMessurier did not hesitate to take the fall. After reviewing Hartley's work over and over again, he called on Alan Davenport, the director of the Boundary Layer Wind Tunnel Laboratory at the University of Western Ontario, to do an extra layer of analysis. Davenport found that, had it not been for the mass damper, a powerful storm as typically experienced once every sixteen years could potentially topple the building. Even so, his assessment showed that the bolts were still not primed to hold, and that there was a real risk of a collapse every fifty-five years, but even more of a case for disaster if the electricity went out before the winds hit the building, taking out the tuned mass damper and everything that had been created to buffer the tower from a storm.

It was July 31, 1978, and the hurricane season started on August 1.

LeMessurier recognized that Hartley was right, but he had no idea what to do to fix the problem. Suicide was an option he considered, Morgenstern reported, but the engineer eventually concluded that there was a better way, a more ethical way, to come to terms with his mistake.

Consulting with Stubbins, he called a meeting with Citicorp and braced for the worst. The issue, however, wasn't so much about taking the fall for the building but getting Citicorp executives in the door and ensuring that they understood the scope of what needed to happen. After days of pushing, LeMessurier was able to sit down with Citicorp's executive vice president, John S. Reed, and put his cards, and $2 million of his own money, on the table. Stubbins was off the hook, but LeMessurier would possibly be bankrupted in fixing what he started. Finally convincing the bank to assist in managing the problem under his leadership, LeMessurier hired an engineering and construction team to work 24/7, surreptitiously, until every bolt was replaced and every corner of the chevron structure was covered in reinforced steel plates. He hired three different weather tracking offices to provide him with daily updates.

At 6:30 in the morning, a month after the work started, Hurricane Ella was skimming the coast, and LeMessurier and the city had to decide whether or not to evacuate the core of Manhattan. The colossal retrofit wasn't finished, but the most critical challenges in the design on the thirtieth floor of the building had been managed first. It was a breath-holding event, but as Ella changed course and bypassed New York, the sun came out and LeMessurier could weather on.

This is not a cybersecurity story. It is, however, a story about accountability, and one that sheds light on what most business leadership teams have to contend with over the course of their history: massive challenges that threaten to take them, their clients and customers, and their community down. The Citicorp tower still stands, many decades later, because of the brilliance of Hartley, the commitment of LeMessurier, and the rallying of a community that aimed to do the right thing. They could have chanced it, or they could have just taken the whole building down. They could have watched it fall, destroying lives and livelihoods.

Doing the right thing, and doing the thing right

The critical thing to learn from this story is not about engineering. It's not even about LeMessurier and his arrogance, or his financial comeuppance. This story is about doing the right thing, making hard choices, and working with a team of professionals. Each of these professionals was responsible for their part of the solution, though very few of them had the individual knowledge to understand what exactly had gone wrong in the first place. This is why the Citicorp tower story is important: it was not simply an engineering problem for an engineer to solve, it was a business risk for everyone in the business to manage.

Cybersecurity is likewise not an IT problem to solve. It is a business risk to manage.

Putting automated cybersecurity systems in place provides only a false sense of security. That's because systems are far from being the only thing you need to do to keep your company safe. Systems aren't even the most important thing. Even those at the top of the company can be stalked, targeted, and harpooned without any virtual walls being breached. Yes, IT is important, but your IT security can only work when there is a strategic, C-suite level plan in place for security that integrates IT with risk management at all levels of the company.

Let's look at why this is the case in real terms. In 2014, Canadian security organization eSentire discovered a persistent attack that targeted senior executives in New York hedge funds. Nearly sixteen months after eSentire reported the campaign to the U.S. Securities and Exchange Commission (SEC), the scam was attributed to the organized crime group FIN4. They had targeted individuals at nearly one hundred global companies that had access to sensitive, not-yet-public merger and acquisition information. The attackers knew who they were targeting and used deep investment tactics, now referred to as hands-on-keyboard, to infiltrate their stable of victims. As is often the case, criminals hijack legitimate documents (in this case, a tax document) as the bait. The Microsoft Word document also contained a macro that, upon opening, downloaded a credential harvesting tool that mimicked a Windows login screen, and even contained the target organization's logo. Hackers then used the compromised credentials of a senior executive to send the infected document to a colleague at another organization.

In this way, FIN4 moved through one organization at a time until they had compromised seventy organizations. They had access to trillions of dollars in funds scattered across the public markets. This sum of money ran close to the same amount that toppled global economies in the wake of the 2008 sub-prime market collapse, or the economic instability attributed to the COVID-19 outbreak.

FIN4 aren't fly-by-night hackers. Like many other organized criminal organizations, they speak English fluently. They understand how businesses and legal firms work with the knowledge of experts. And they know exactly how to get insider information because they know how to engage in the kind of networking practices that are common in circles that rely on LinkedIn pages to get a sense of who's on the other end of the call. These attackers pose as IT support workers, deal advisors, financial experts, and lawyers, and seek out disgruntled employees to act as data sources, but they also go right to the top. They can schmooze their ways into corporate circles with ease, and then go right for the payday: they obtain access to a company's system through a privileged account, where they install surveillance hooks to gather valuable undisclosed information. This not only can make them millions, if not billions of dollars, but it can also change the way that our entire financial systems work (more on that later).

And these risks are just as prevalent for smaller organizations as for large ones. Spear phishing, where individuals up the value chain are targeted for larger wins, can pay off for smaller-scale organized crime and individuals.

Let's take the example of a managing partner at a Manhattan firm. One of her work responsibilities was purchasing art, which she had a habit of doing on her lunch breaks on public Wi-Fi. Instead of hacking into her bank account or directly into her email, a cybercrime syndicate located her iTunes credentials. Through that portal, they were able to tap into her Gmail account and change the password, redirecting the notifications elsewhere and deleting any evidence they were there. They found, very quickly, several emails from an art dealer and the number of transactions that were taking place between the partner and the art company. Immediately, they set up a fake art dealer website domain that looked exactly like the one that the company used. In fact, they used two *n*'s side-by-side to mimic the *m* in the domain name so that it wouldn't look much different from the real thing. A quick pass at the site, and you'd never know the difference. And she didn't. They were able to pull catalog information and build very authentic-looking invoices.

The fake art site began emailing invoices to the company, and at the same time, intercepting and deleting the real invoices in her email inbox. The partner's firm paid out nearly $400,000 in fake invoices until, a couple of months later, she got a call from the real art company. But the damage was done.

Fraud of another matter embroiled the CEOs of two rival companies. Jide Zeitlin, the founder of a private equity firm and CEO of a wireless telecommunications tower business, was accused of posing as the CEO of his rival, American Tower, to send a rather negative CNN article to two of American Tower's investors.[2] The CEO of American Tower was vindicated through the legal process, and it cost Zeitlin far more than he could have expected. Nearly a decade later, Zeitlin was the Obama administration's nominee to lead the U.S. interests in financial reform of the United Nations. Although approved by the Senate, he later withdrew his nomination based on "personal reasons," but his business dealings, including impersonating the CEO of his rival, came under heavy scrutiny.[3]

In most cases, cyber risk decisions fail to make the desk of the CEO or board.[4] And, all too often, the security leader only reports to the board after a security incident impacts the business.

Strategic risk management isn't about ones and zeros

Cybersecurity has to become part of a bigger conversation, connecting risks like these to strategic planning. In the average company, other than putting some technological stopgaps in place, usually risk isn't truly assessed until a security event takes place. People, even in leadership positions, remain blissfully ignorant because they think that they are too small to target. They turn a blind eye, hoping for plausible deniability. Or, like Hartley, LeMessurier, and Citicorp, you can work hard to mitigate risk and take responsibility as soon as possible. If you don't, your story is the one that ends up on the twenty-four-hour news cycle.

A cybersecurity event that targeted Travelex in December 2019 illustrates how poor communication can lead to a massive PR failure. The foreign exchange company based in London found that several of their regional sites were under siege. The attack resulted in a company-wide system outage, forcing employees back to pen and paper to laboriously complete currency exchange transactions. The company elected to post a misleading maintenance notice on several of their later-disabled websites. It wasn't until weeks later that the company admitted the outage was not due to scheduled maintenance but was the result of malicious cyberattacks that simultaneously crippled their critical business systems and stole client data for resale on the dark web. But the criminal attack didn't stop there. On top of the massive (and likely extremely costly) operational disruption, the criminals then demanded a multimillion-dollar fee to not publish customer records, causing a massive data breach and subsequent investigation and likely penalties under the European General Data Protection Regulation (GDPR) privacy laws. In this case, the criminals understood the fiduciary responsibilities of the organization and used privacy penalties as a lever to extort the company further.

But the weak link in this kind of crime is also physical rather than virtual. Hackers often gain a great deal of access to the means into accounts even through the purchase of physical data, such as leaked passwords and identities of a number of key company representatives, which allow them to then create more robust pathways to infiltrating large-scale systems. In reality this means that the way in which we have typically dealt with identity theft offline is also relevant to dealing with attacks online. Companies and individuals still have to be vigilant about the way in which they develop a protection protocol for their physical assets, because these can be easily stolen.

It has long been said that the chief security officer is the least interesting person to the board until they become the most interesting person—usually after a major security incident. Boards, and everyone else, need to take more interest in them, sooner.

To start, every company has to be able to answer one question: what is your risk? It's not a simple question to answer. Several elements have to be assessed on an ongoing basis—and not just the one time—for safety to be assured. These include the creation and use of technological applications; people and the ways in which they access information; and processes, policies, guidelines, and business strategies that may create inroads for hackers.

The plan to address your risk is a whole other ballgame.

And the press, the public, and government and law enforcement investigators recognize a fact that many business leaders still don't. You can't simply blame a massive breach with significant impact on customers on a single IT control. An unpatched server, a misconfigured network router, or an unmonitored "bad apple" employee is not where the buck stops. Now we have to ask why businesses didn't budget for patch management tools that would have prevented an out-of-date server from turning into a culprit that brought down operations. And we have to check why we didn't have monitoring and fundamental user controls that would have flagged bad apples in the bunch. We're talking about a new world of work in which investigators, and the court of public opinion, follow the money to the board. Did the board know how and why their risk exposure was high enough for a breach to take place? Did they allocate the necessary budget and resources to protect their business from predators? Did they know what questions to ask and answers to receive to determine whether their business was adequately protected?

Everyone is a part of the conversation, and everyone is responsible.

What we know now, based on what insurers, law enforcement, and the public expects, is that companies have to achieve key deliverables. What can you do?

- Does your board have access to security expertise and receive regular reporting from the security team?

- Does your team document your registry of assets and data that must remain protected, along with a list of likely scenarios in which this data could be compromised?

- Is everyone prepared to ensure that proper practices and execution of policies are in place?

- Are there sound controls of people, process, and technology that can be used as checks and balances on a daily basis?

- Have you completed an analysis of risk on a time-sensitive basis and also as routine in each level of the organization?

- Have you created acceptable alternatives that can be put into place if a breach takes place?

- Have you produced implementation guidelines that allow different arms of the company to engage in using these protocols?

- Do you have a method to test company and individual compliance against the framework before and after breaches?

- And finally, have you established a commitment to ongoing documentation as a regular part of every step in the process?

There are several good guides on the key pillars of risk management and board obligations: the National Association of Corporate Directors (NACD) cyber risk oversight guide,[5] the National Cyber Security Centre board toolkit,[6] and *Navigating the Digital Age*.[7] While each resource provides differing levels of information, there are five common pillars:

- **AWARENESS:** understanding the impact of cyber risks and trends, experiencing the business impact of a breach, and exposing personal risks

- **RISK:** identifying nonpublic assets and protected data, and documenting regulatory and contractual obligations

- **PROGRAM:** establishing budget, staffing, and programs that align to overall business risk priorities

- **REPORTING:** annual planning, quarterly reporting, dashboards, and peer/industry comparisons of performance

- **INCIDENTS:** understanding incident response, board roles, critical business decisions, and reporting to authorities and crisis communications

That's a lot of steps. And a lot of risk analysis, protocol, and checks and balances that have to take place every day, month, and year. Cybersecurity requires everyone in the company to take part, not just to meet basic standards of compliance, but to be proactive.

But that's not just it. It's not just about ones and zeros, the binary code that separates people from computers.

What we're looking at, right here and right now, is something that transcends technology. It's a whole new world where you have to protect yourself not only from cybercriminals but from the legal and social liability that can be tied to not protecting your company enough in the first place. And corporate cyber service providers, like customer relationship management, communication, and project management software companies, are pushing more responsibility for security onto their users because differences in user behavior and their attendant security risks are at the heart of most breaches.

The problem is that some of these breaches are bigger, and affect more people, than we've ever expected. The threat is looming large, and we're only going to have to become more aware, more vigilant, and more creative in how we keep the enemy from walking right in the front door, briefcase in hand.

3

YOU'RE GOING TO
NEED A BIGGER BOAT

RAUL VEGA NEEDED to buy his way out of Costa Gravas.* For years, he had been making enough money through his oil industry investments to raise the hackles of the barely elected politicians who had a stranglehold over his home country's government. But that wasn't the only reason he had to leave. Vega was outspoken about the fact that there were more lies than truths, and he had the audacity to criticize the current administration's policies and to expose their illegal operations and violent means of controlling the population. These actions made doing business in Costa Gravas very difficult.

Vega was trying, or so he thought, to bring his country into a modern, globalized business community through legal business development, legitimately elected governments, and pushing back against generations of gray-market hegemony. He believed that his work would raise the GDP and the

---

* Not his actual name; not a real country.

standard of living, not only through his own businesses but through his investments in a number of local start-ups. He had been quietly moving his money into foreign banks and tax havens for several years already, as oil prices increased by more than 860 percent in the last twenty years, leading to a significant increase in his earnings. Vega thought his financial power would shield him and that he could leverage his vast wealth to make the right kind of waves, ones that would nudge the government into seeing things his way.

For his troubles, the Costa Gravas government labeled him a dissident and enemy of the state.

Let's say that, because of its poor fiscal and monetary management, the fictional country of Costa Gravas ranked last out of all countries for the perceived quality of its institutions, reflecting the business sector's enduring concerns about the weak rule of law, government inefficiencies, and the government's lack of evenhandedness in its dealings with the private sector. Attempts by the private sector to collaborate with the government to improve these conditions simply were not working, and the unrest was getting worse daily. In fact, the nation's president created a foreign policy environment that led to doubling the royalties paid by foreign corporations who participated in oil development partnerships in Costa Gravas, which means that no one was leaving with their investments intact, even the largest of American organizations that snapped up significant oil assets there in the 1980s.

It's no wonder Vega needed to get out. Stuck in a legal emigration hellscape, unable to secure a permanent place to land in Canada or in the United States, he retained one of the largest and most experienced immigration law firms in the world, Donner Reynolds, to take his case.† Things were in process.

---

† Again, a pseudonym.

Vega's lawyers were moving quickly, and he had every hope of finding safe harbor somewhere else.

What no one expected was that Vega would become a moving target and his home country's government would use any means to pursue and punish him. When the Costa Gravas government discovered that Vega had fled the country, wealth in hand, they took the unexpected step of publicly targeting him with an open statement to the world. They took to social media and publicly threatened that anyone who helped him would be severely punished.

What can a country like Costa Gravas do in this situation, realistically? With little international reach or political allegiances, Costa Gravas wasn't about to physically target Vega on another country's soil. Yet Vega's actions were intolerable and had to be visibly quashed to discourage others from following his outspoken ways.

Countries don't need bullets, polonium-laced cocktails, or poison-tipped umbrellas to exact revenge. In the online world, everyone has a threat surface littered with digital vulnerabilities. What's true for basement hackers with chips on their shoulders is just as true for foreign presidents angry about petulant business leaders like Vega. State-sponsored cybercrime, like all other forms of cybercrime, is only becoming more pervasive. Costa Gravas's gray economy, fueled by multilateral economic sanctions from around the world, allows it to act with impunity when comes to hacking. And the same holds true for other nations. Military might is often asymmetrical and reserved for the biggest players. But in a cyber war, even underdog nations like Costa Gravas or North Korea can muster a digital arsenal that rivals that of Western nations or even China.

Like countless hacks before it, it started with a seemingly innocuous email. But this time the hackers' method of getting in was much more sophisticated. A legal clerk at Donner

Reynolds received information that aligned with the firm's case file on Vega. In fact, a quick scan of the email would never have revealed that it was a phishing spoof, even to someone trained to pick up on common hacks. It contained insider knowledge of the case (including the document management system tracking number) and referenced the Donner Reynolds internal file transfer system (used to move files too big for email). This kind of information can be harvested or scammed much earlier from another arm of the large firm so that this request would go undetected, or it can even be purchased on the dark web.

The clerk clicked on the false link to the file transfer system, and the Costa Gravas national assigned to this case jumped right into Donner Reynolds's virtual private network (VPN). Most businesses use one or more VPN to encrypt communications and thereby securely move data across geographical locations and from remote employees (this is often commonly referred to as encrypting "data in motion").

When the clerk entered their credentials into the false link provided in the phishing email, the hackers captured (often referred to as "harvesting") legitimate access to the firm's network. And as more often than not, most employees use common credentials (usernames and passwords) across multiple corporate systems (think email, VPN, file servers, and so on).

Using these legitimate employee credentials, the hackers then used the firm's own administrative tools to move around the network. All businesses rely on administrative tools (like Microsoft's Remote Desktop Protocol or operating system command-line tools like PowerShell) to remotely access online network systems. It's a necessary risk in a distributed world, and a practice operated in almost every company.

The hackers used PowerShell to move around the network, create new users with administrative authority, disable security systems, snoop email servers, and so on. They had the key to the kingdom. They could steal their entire client database, or shut down Donner Reynolds's network and send them back into the proverbial internet stone age, all while drinking their first cup of coffee.

Just like that.

Always be skeptical

Think about it for a moment. Most of us, even those with a tiny semblance of an understanding of cybersecurity, know that when you get an email with a link in it, you don't click on the link. For example, when you receive an email or text message purportedly from your bank, you don't click on the supplied link. Rather, you log into the bank's site independently and verify the communication. In this case, with the added layer of espionage that went into planning for this hack, and with the detailed knowledge that the Costa Gravas nationals laid out like a cappuccino bar in front of a tired and busy law clerk, Donner Reynolds experienced something that they didn't expect. The clerk gave the hacker full privileges because they trusted the information in the email, and because the law firm was so large that clerks regularly received and sent similar emails to other employees whom they didn't personally know.

In essence, Donner Reynolds had let the hackers in, right through the employee entrance, and held the door open for them.

There were no witnesses to the hackers' quick and steady movements through the law firm's endless files of confidential information. Everything that occurred looked like a legitimate activity, at least in the beginning. Because of their VPN access, the hackers didn't need to continue logging in as the clerk, which would have been a giveaway to the firm's tech team. Right away, the Costa Gravas nationals were able create new, official Donner Reynolds users in the system and, in doing so, gave themselves system administrator privileges. With an organization that large, the hackers' tracks were very difficult to trace, because the new users could easily have been new employees at any Donner Reynolds location around the globe. They were also able to install a script on the email server, which collected information based on specific accounts and keywords.

What happened next was even more unexpected, because the hackers weren't targeting Raul Vega, and they weren't aiming to take down the law firm either.

The hackers were going after the attorneys engaged in Vega's case. Their goal? Not to kill, but to compromise. The hackers wanted to drag Vega's lawyers to the edge of a high cliff, one that they would have to jump off unless they submitted to the hackers' whims. There would be no painless way out.

Let's talk about some of the ways that a lawyer, or anyone for that matter, could get compromised. Once hackers break into a system and have administrative access, they can read all your emails. Every single one. If they search for the word "divorce" in a law firm's email server, hackers might get a massive dump of useless files. It's easy to get mired in a level of detailed data. If, on the other hand, they search for "my divorce," the hackers might just find something useful, like a despondent email from a lawyer to a friend about a personal custody battle with an ex-spouse. That small piece of information can be spun into gold to a creative hacker, who could threaten that same lawyer with interference in the divorce, perhaps revealing hidden assets or secret affairs. The result could be the permanent loss of the target's financial equity in the divorce, or even their children. Lawyers could be compelled to follow hackers' instructions, just like the parent of a kidnapped child in a Liam Neeson film, if they are vulnerable in any way. Is their credit at risk? Do they have a substance abuse problem? Any personal risk that a lawyer carries is a legal firm risk.

And there's another darker, more fear-inducing side to this story. Hackers can also plant information. Imagine what kind of illicit photographs or videos a hacker could put on some-body's laptop that could destroy their job, send them to jail, or end their marriage, to ensure that they comply with an active threat. Whatever distant fear keeps you up at night worrying, from your personal wealth to a private fetish, can be repli-cated with ease in a digital space. When you're an experienced hacker, reputational assassination is a good way to get what you want.

So why wasn't Donner Reynolds prepared for this risk? It's clear that they were dealing with very determined and moti-vated hackers willing to go right over the edge, which was a risk for which they couldn't calculate ahead of time. We're not only talking about criminal activity but unconscionable and unpredictable actions. Many people feel secure in their belief that hacking is innocuous, that most of the time it's more Robin Hood than Rasputin. In skilled criminal hands, however, it's soul-destroying, life-crushing, cold-blooded work. These Costa Gravas hackers understood the culture of the legal indus-try, and they were only too willing to dig deep into a series of individual lives to take down everyone that stood between their government and Raul Vega.

The business of cybercrime takes time, patience, skill, and a tolerance for the monotonous, but it cuts right to the heart of who we are, and what we are willing to give up in order to protect ourselves and others.

However, many of us think that our companies don't have anything worth stealing, or worse, that we're a small fish in a big pond, and therefore we're not at risk. Neither is true: there are no longer any demographic limitations on who will be targeted.

Criminals target by IP address, not zip code

Law firms are a good case in point. Even when they are a part of small- or medium-sized firms, lawyers are deeply connected to businesses and people who have access to large sums of money. They manage confidential information that can be damaging or used to illegally profit through the buying and selling of stock on public markets. Although not every firm represents clients like Raul Vega, the legal industry is the crossroads of our economy. They help craft the same legislation they interpret for clients. They write the deals that bring investment money to businesses that develop tomorrow's products. And they have unparalleled access to our private lives in terms of estate planning, real estate transactions, and divorces.

Certain practices make the criminal connection of the dots more straightforward. For example, some lawyers specialize in managing money for high-wealth individuals and their families. Others in tax havens shelter money for the rich and famous, politicians, and in the rare case, even alleged criminals. These firms have been doing this for generations, with some firms' records going back hundreds of years. Donner Reynolds was founded in the United States in the nineteenth century. They were established and confident in their work and their risk management. They had layers of cybersecurity already in place, and people trained on every floor of their multiple global office locations. They had systems, they had practices, and they had risk management protocols for cybersecurity in place, and all of these failed them. Why? Because there will always be a way to get in the door when you don't think like a hacker.

And it's not just Donner Reynolds. They weren't negligent. But they were misguided in thinking that they couldn't be a target. Yet law firms are a popular target of cyber criminals. Unfortunately, most firms suffer in silence and these attacks never go noticed nor make the headlines.

The first public bloody nose came in 2016 when an attack on Wall Street law firms Cravath, Swaine & Moore LLP and Weil, Gotshal & Manges LLP demonstrated how stolen Food and Drug Administration (FDA) filings and press releases could be used to make millions of dollars in illegal stock trades. The Paradise Papers and Panama Papers demonstrated that hackers could monetize or weaponize even innocuous tax law files. Ransomware attacks collected a pirate's bounty in payments, cost a small fortune in lost billable hours, and did untold damage to many firms' reputations. Today, ransoms are morphing into extortion as hackers demand payment to avoid exposure of damaging information.

Still, most attacks go unnoticed by the public. And these attacks show an uncanny understanding of the inner workings of the industry. Back in 2016, hundreds of law firms fell to ransomware attacks carried in emails that purported to come from their specific state bar associations. The campaigns plagued many East Coast law firms, and their peers across the country in Texas and Florida. Most of the emails carried an emotive subject line like "A complaint has been filed against your business" or "See you in court" and demanded a rebuttal within ten days. The email originating from statesattorney@ outlook.com (a dead giveaway since all government agencies use the .gov domain) contained a PDF of the alleged complaint. Once opened, the PDF launched a small program that called home to the hacker servers and downloaded multiple malware packages, including ransomware. One victim firm lost twenty years of client records. Another lost $500,000 in billable hours related to disrupted court cases.

In another attack, a ten-attorney firm in Rhode Island was hit by similar ransomware that led to months of repair and cost the firm (according to their calculations) $700,000 in billable hours. As we will discuss in greater detail in chapter 9, the firm, Moses Afonso Ryan, sued Sentinel Risk Insurance Group in 2017, claiming the insurer breached its contract by refusing to pay the lost revenue under business income interruption coverage.

Wire transfer scams are also common for law firms: a hacker can take advantage of insider knowledge about long-standing wire-transfer relationships with a firm's suppliers or customers, and can change account details to their benefit. In 2019, Dentons Canada LLP sued Trisura Guarantee Insurance Company after a firm employee fell victim to a scam and paid out $2.5 million in fraudulent wire transfers to banks in Hong Kong. While the firm recovered $800,000, the insurer did not consider the loss the result of fraud and refused to cover the $1.7 million gap.

In one case I worked, criminals stole the customer database of a large law firm to send invoices to their clients. The invoices were fake, but linked back to legitimate work and referenced authentic case tracking file numbers. When clients called to complain about double-billing for paid services rendered, the firm realized that criminals outside the firm possessed accounting information, and the resulting cleanup with customers did a number on their reputation and strained client relations to the breaking point.

In a more recent attack, a very devious cybercriminal posed as a Harvard law student to gain the trust of several lawyers at the target firm and then emailed the firm partners a fake school survey. Once opened, the Microsoft Office document launched a macro that downloaded multiple malware payloads.

For law firms that don't think they have anything worth stealing, they do seem to have a lot to lose.

All of these attacks are forms of social engineering.

What it comes down to is that, far from being stereotypically antisocial, hackers excel at using psychological manipulation to trick people into divulging confidential information or providing access to funds, and creating a novel, fear-based economy that has only started to reveal itself. Starting with lawyers' and other employees' LinkedIn, Facebook, and other social accounts, they can find a wealth of information, including contact information, connections, friends, ongoing business deals, and more. And this can happen just as much at the top of companies as on the front ranks. According to FBI statistics from 2019, CEO fraud is now a $26 billion scam,[1] with top executives and administrators targeted because they are less likely than other employees to understand the risks and ramifications of responding to emails without the proper care. Many CEOs believe that if an email gets through to their desk, it's automatically safe, but that's far from true.

Raul Vega and Donner Reynolds survived their hack, but not before substantial damage was done to the firm. Luckily, the attack was detected by their contracted security firm, which spent the first twelve hours locked in duel with the attackers, tracking their movements, and playing whack-a-mole to keep them kicked out of the law firm's network. At one point, the law firm disabled all remote access. The aftermath included the services of an incident response firm to determine motive and potential damage and gather the evidence handed over to law enforcement and coordinated government agencies.

The fact is that it's not just Costa Gravas. Many struggling nations will continue to ramp up their cyber proficiencies, and this may very well change the status quo of what we expect from our interactions and systems. These events may trigger an even more extreme political domino effect, where nations begin to further cut themselves off from the world simply because they can. "Costa Gravas will create a cryptocurrency," backed by oil, gas, gold, and diamond reserves, President Augusto Elgrande said in one of his regular Sunday televised broadcasts in late 2018, a five-hour showcase of Navidad songs and dancing. The new *petro* currency, he said, would help Costa Gravas "advance in issues of monetary sovereignty, to make financial transactions and overcome the financial blockade." With those new resources, leaning into the benefits of digital transactions and gray business models, hacking may very well become a major part of the core competencies of Costa Gravas, and other similarly impoverished nations. It's a vicious cycle. They hack to make money, and the money fuels more competent and skilled hacking. As they become more proficient and successful, they earn more money, and thus leverage criminal hacking as a reliable revenue stream. And so on around the cyber merry-go-round. It's much easier than staging military forces and equipment and sending them into a bloody and costly battle.

When all is said and done, and when we explore the overlapping layers of social change that have predicated the Vega case, it seems almost impossible to protect yourself, your organization, and your clients from this psychologically insidious and strategically motivated level of cybercrime. A company can devote enormous resources to cybersecurity, do everything right, and still be vulnerable to a breach when it is attacked by a nation-state or an advanced cybercriminal or group. That's because these criminals' actions are not simply predicated by their own propensity for breaking the rules.

But you can decrease your vulnerability.

You're going to need a bigger boat

As actor Roy Scheider (in the role of police chief Martin Brody) quips after seeing the great white in director Steven Spielberg's 1975 blockbuster thriller, *Jaws*, "You're gonna need a bigger boat."

One of the most quotable lines in movie history, it wasn't in the script. And this movie reference is more relevant to this story of cybersecurity than it may first appear. Carl Gottlieb, one of the screenplay's writers and an original scribe on ABC's *The Odd Couple*, spoke with the *Hollywood Reporter* in 2016 about how the line came to represent the film. Because much of *Jaws* was filmed on the water, all of the equipment for the shoot was housed on a barge nicknamed the USS *Garage Sale*.[2] The film's producers were known for their tight purse strings, and only shelled out for a tiny dinghy to move expensive equipment, and even to film critical scenes. The fact that they needed a bigger boat became an in-joke on the set, especially when the swells were rocking the camera and Spielberg couldn't get his shot.

"You're gonna need a bigger boat" became the catchphrase for the beleaguered crew. When they shot the scene in which Brody gets a look at the shark for the first time, Scheider dropped in the line.

The same thing is true for companies assessing their risk. We all have to build a bigger boat. It's not just that the sharks are bigger than we expected. It's that we're unable to perform critical functions well unless we have a proportionate budget to sail the industry seas we choose. Even small companies have big-company problems when it comes to cybercrime. We have to create an approach to preventing cybercrime that focuses less on the single and simplistic issue of the ones and zeros in our systems, and more on the holistic nature of risk. We need a boat with room for more than one camera lens, the one that is trained on our data and virtual assets. What the Vega story reveals is that risk management involves securing every aspect of your ecosystem, not just remote connections and servers. Employees get duped, and preventative measures get compromised or sidestepped. Unless you're really, truly paying attention, and trying to find patterns in the noise of everyday business, these risks will overcome the average company. And finding the needle in the cyber haystack is the easy part (relatively speaking)—you must know what to do with the needle *if* you find it. In the case of Donner Reynolds, a novel machine-learning algorithm detected subtle patterns in the remote commands in PowerShell and flagged the suspicious activity to a team of trained security analysts who dug in, investigated in real time, and battled to stop it before it became business disrupting. Or worse.

We will never know or be able to predict all cybersecurity risks. They are as variable as the number of ideas in the minds of the most creative, talented, and funded criminals in our midst. And these criminals infiltrate the most carefully protected cyber fortresses because they prey on people, not systems.

Systems do count, in some ways. In this case, multiple security gates and mechanisms would have prevented or at least slowed the nation-state attack. In cybersecurity, the principle of least privilege requires that in a computing environment, every module (such as a process, a user, or a program) must be able to access only what is necessary for its legitimate purpose. In this case, network segmentation and least privilege would have stopped attackers from creating new users with top administrative privileges that could disable systems and access critical infrastructure like the email server. Multifactor authentication would have delayed the unauthorized use on the compromised credentials because the attacker would need additional devices or information to gain access through the VPN. Comprehensive logging would have enabled quicker detection and response. IP range and country blocking (called geofencing) would have delayed attackers and forced alternate launch points. Employees used personal devices (called Bring Your Own Device, or BYOD), which were not managed. Again, another contributing factor to the attack. And of course, employee security awareness training is imperative. Yes, the phishing lure was well crafted, but multiple employees received it.

Because, as we've seen, the big problem isn't systems, it's people.

Our business mindset must shift from security as an IT problem to solve (and cost to minimize) to that of enterprise risk management. It's about building a communication chain that links the top of the organization with everyone participating in the ecosystem. This full-stack alignment is critical to establishing a corporate culture that understands risk mitigation and doesn't view security as an inconvenience or a necessary evil.

Let's consider the Donner Reynolds story again. We could ask if the organization should have taken on Vega's case. After all, right or wrong, as a client he exposed the organization to a hot zone of political radioactivity. And no organization should be expected to combat a nation-state attack. That said, few organizations are going to turn down a lucrative client.

So, what can an organization like this do if they do take on a case like this one? How can they mitigate the risk associated with that kind of reward?

Security needs a seat at the table alongside the general counsel when a big case changes the status quo. But also, think about how a law firm, or any company, communicates what they are doing between departments. The tax practice may have no idea what the criminal practice is up to. In fact, so-called Chinese walls between departments may actually be required to slow down knowledge transfer for legal reasons. Fair enough. But what the company could do is start with preemptive communications to all employees. A simple email could go out stating that the firm was taking on a new client who brings an element of risk associated with a specific nation-state, asking all employees to remain hypervigilant and report any aberrant behavior or suspicious emails. A review of the security awareness training available would also be a good idea.

Next, as the attack spread and IT sprang into action, critical decisions needed to be made. Take, for instance, the IT recommendation to disable remote access for hundreds of employees. Senior attorneys and junior support staff alike would be cut off from core services they rely upon to serve their clients, which would mean that they wouldn't react kindly, and could block IT from doing their jobs. That's a contentious decision that needs the backing of the partners and active communication from their desks. Managing partners need to make those kinds of calls because they are critical to the reputation and financial health of the business. So why is IT security confined to a closet and ignored most of the time? Remember as we've already discussed, the IT team is the least interesting part of the organization until it becomes the most interesting, and that's not where we want to be.

Now consider external communications. Should the firm tell the client? Well, that seems obvious. But, should other clients be notified? In the United States, the American Bar Association published Formal Opinion 483 in late 2018 that covers lawyers' obligations in the event of an electronic data breach, which states that lawyers have the obligation to notify clients even if they have not been affected.[3] Legal obligations aside, there are issues of trust, and respecting the safety and considerations of the client. It's a gray area, but erring on the side of caution can prevent bigger consequences down the road.

What about calling law enforcement? The law firm was attacked and broken into. That's the domain of the legal quarterback or general counsel. What triggers exist? What information matters, and when do we pull the alarm? In doing so, how do we work with law enforcement going forward and how will this impact the business?

Security is no longer an IT expense to manage. It's a key pillar of any risk management plan. Firms and businesses must document risks and known obligations, and be able to consistently articulate which risks they mitigate through security controls, which risks they can reduce or offset through other measures (such as carrying cyber insurance), and which ones they have to accept as a part of doing business. And is the case in most practitioner-based businesses like accounting, law, or medicine, high-ranking employees are extended network privileges like administrative rights. But rank does not correlate to privilege. Think "need to know." Most people don't need to know.

In many cases, implementing specific security controls can eliminate or at least slow attackers and create tripwires that flag their presence. What can you do?

- Have you eliminated administrative rights to all but administrators?

- Have you eliminated name-based (first.last@firm.com) credentials for those requiring administrative rights, and implemented dual approval before changes can be made to critical security or network systems?

- Do you require encryption at both rest and in motion (so, encrypted drives and VPNs) to access corporate systems?

- Do you employ endpoint and data loss prevention defenses that flag when user devices are modified in unusual ways (like having AV disabled), or when users are modifying restricted documents?

- Can you deploy mobile device management or enterprise device management to restrict network access from personal devices, or limit access to critical systems?

One thing is for sure. Chief Brody had it right. You are going to need a bigger boat. In our world you're not hunting the shark. The sharks are hunting you. And, like areas populated with sharks in real life, we cannot conquer the species in the virtual world, but we can take down the ones we see. Even so, there are always other predators below the surface, and they know that smaller organizations make a worthwhile meal just the same as the big ones.

4

ONLY FROM DISASTER
CAN WE BE RESURRECTED

IN **1983, A** just-out-of-the-box Boeing 767 ran out of fuel mid-flight.

Air Canada Flight 143 was making its regular route between Montreal and Edmonton in good time, an easy jump of just over two thousand miles of open, northern skies at 41,000 feet, when the crew alerting system went off.

Twice.

A 767 has two engines, one under each wing. Four beeps in quick succession told the crew that there was a problem with the fuel pressure in the left engine. The crew checked the flight management computer, which showed more than ample fuel to make their destination. There was a low possibility that the brand-new fuel pump had failed. More likely, they were dealing with an intermittent computer glitch. Even so, Captain Bob Pearson and First Officer Maurice Quintal followed procedures and switched off the fuel pump. Gravity would ensure that fuel continued to flow to the engine, and pilots train in simulators for just this type of event. Pearson and Quintal calmly went about preparing for a single-engine landing. But, just after they had silenced the first alarm and diagnosed the suspected problem, a second alarm broke the returned calm in the cockpit. The warning alarm signified that all engines were out. The pilots later recalled never having heard this "long bong" sound before. Now the right engine was reporting a fuel pressure problem. A few seconds later, starved of fuel, both Pratt & Whitney engines flamed out.

None of this should have happened. This new aircraft represented the next generation in civil aviation engineering. Passenger air travel was moving into the digital age. Fully electronic avionics, referred to as a glass cockpit, had replaced World War II–era mechanical instruments, and fly-by-wire computer-controlled actuators moved flight control surfaces and throttled engines, replacing obsolete cable and pulley systems. But why did the fuel gauge show that the tanks were empty? The 767 was also the first generation of glass cockpits equipped with a computer-based fuel system. This system had well-documented intermittent issues and the manufacturer published a service bulletin describing the issues and providing a workaround for flight crews and pilot. This same issue was reported by the previous flight crew on the aircraft, and Pearson was aware, well ahead of time, that the fuel computer would be disabled. That's why, before the flight, he had ordered the ground crew to confirm an adequate fuel level using a float stick. It sounds like what it is: a dipstick lowered into the fuel tanks in the wings to measure fuel load the way you'd check the oil level in your car's engine.

Here's where things got murky. At the time, Canada was switching from the old British imperial measurement system to the metric system. The ground crew had miscalculated fuel quantities while making imperial-to-metric conversions on the fly, and the pilots didn't catch the error. The flight had departed a stop in Ottawa with about half of the required fuel, and no working fuel computer system to flag the problem.

The error wasn't one of technology, or lack of planning, but basic math.

The passengers were finishing their dinner, and unbeknownst to them, the 140-tonne aircraft was on its way down. As the plane descended through 35,000 feet, the copilot searched their emergency manuals and checklists for the procedure to deal with total engine loss. No such protocol existed. Without power, the digital flight panels switched off, leaving just a few basic emergency-powered instruments.

Sometimes, human error isn't really error, it's bias

In his book *The Field Guide to Understanding 'Human Error'*, Sidney Dekker argues that physical human error is often the target of blame when the reality of our actions may be affected by many different overlapping factors.[1] When faced with a security breach or emergency, we may stop an investigation short of examining factors that led directly to the choices we make, like what's happening in our environment, employer policies, employee training, security controls, social and economic requirements, political and workplace pressures, budget and resourcing decisions, and many more interconnected factors. These are systemic factors, namely the kinds of issues that influence our decisions but that may not be easily predicted, understood, or prevented.

In the case of the 767, the reason that both engines failed wasn't a lack of training or a lack of planning. That plane was going down because of a lack of familiarity with a new kind of measurement, coupled with the fact that, because of its new computer systems, the 767 required only two flight crew instead of three, which previous generations that required a flight engineer had. Everything was a little bit different, and that cascade of slight differences threw everyone off their game, even though they had all of the recommended checks and balances in place.

Like this aviation story, cybersecurity incidents and data breaches are never the result of a single point of failure, a malicious actor, or simple user error.

So, what is human error really about? Dekker would argue that it often comes down to a set of biases, each of which suggests to us that we know exactly what's going on, when in reality, we don't.

Let's start with what's known as **hindsight bias**. It's our exaggerated ability to feel like we could have predicted and prevented a disaster once we find out both the causes and the outcome. It may seem ludicrous to the average person that we can fly a plane without a serviceable device that reports its current fuel load. That's like driving through the mountains without a gas gauge or any road signs telling us where the next service station is located, and just hoping for the best. But a planned process *is* in place for doing just that, based on how planes were originally fueled up before such gauges were created, and every pilot and engineer knows about it.

When it comes to cybersecurity, similar hindsight biases come into play. We think that an individual ought to know to create technology barriers that make security seamless and fail-proof. But there isn't always a gauge that's going to tell us when a security breach is underway. The factors are too complex and overlapping to really get to the heart of many, if not most, breaches. Like airlines, most industries are eager to adopt technology that lowers operating costs, reduces prices, or increases markets, for example, but then we expect everything to work quickly and immediately, when there are likely going to be operational glitches that we can't predict, whether technological or human.

And let's talk about **outcome bias**. Even more dangerous, outcome bias means that if two people make the same judgment call but get different outcomes, we will judge the one with the worse outcome more harshly. Although IT is often blamed for wanting "toys" or "shiny objects," technology adoption is, more times than not, a business-driven decision. Business leaders are beholden to investors, seek consistent growth, and look to extend the mileage afforded by every dollar, and multiple layers of decisions go into adopting new ways of doing business. Like the 767 in its day, the ubiquitous digitization of every aspect of business drives an ever-increasing adoption of emerging technology. When technology fails, we tend to blame the tech people when they haven't actually done anything differently from what they usually do, which in turn is just part of a larger decision tree.

But emerging technology introduces unknown risk. This means that the tech arms race creates a never-ending flow of new features, approaches, and business models, which produces a nutritious petri dish ideal for misconfiguration and mishandling of these new processes. Yet, this leap-before-looking approach dominates when business requirements force adoption as a means of survival. When no disaster strikes, we don't see too much problem with this. But what happens when things go wrong? We blame the technology, or the people running it, rather than the fact that making tech work is often an iterative process needing care, and more often than not, more time than business leaders want it to.

And that leads us to one additional bias Dekker uncovers: our tendency to focus on the last element in the timeline, or **time bias**. In the 767 story, blame was initially levied on the ground and flight crews for miscalculating fuel loads, because they were the ones doing the last-minute math. Those looking at what happened conveniently ignored all the other factors upstream, like faulty fuel management systems, maintenance errors, and untested operating practices. How many times have we yelled at our TV when the kicker misses the game-winning field goal or the goalie blows the save and our team loses the match? We blame the last event and forget all about the other points that were missed or the goals that were let in.

In a security context, we often see breaches blamed on this idea that there is a single point of failure. For example, let's look at the Equifax breach. This cybersecurity nightmare exposed the personal credit history information of 147 million people in 2017, and the company blamed the breach on an Apache server that was updated improperly. Ultimately, they placed the blame on an IT employee who was probably overworked or possibly undertrained to properly maintain the system, or who didn't have the resources to prevent such things from taking place. But what about the person who refused to fund the kinds of tools that could have automated this process? What about the team leader who didn't listen closely enough when that employee asked for more support or additional technological barriers? It turned out, the Office for Civil Rights in the United States uncovered a Noah's Ark of security gaps that led to the mega breach.[2]

This kind of event highlights our natural desire to over-simplify and encapsulate an event so that we have a clear antagonist upon whom we can heap the blame.

A false sense of security

Bias causes us to miss the issues that directly lead to security breaches in the first place.

Let's take a 2019 Desjardins breach. In that case, the insurance company described the situation as one in which a staffer "shared" personal information of 2.7 million people. They blamed a rogue employee, by inference exonerating their actions and systems, and ignoring everything that they ought to have done to ensure that they had the protection they needed for their clients. But this shouldn't exonerate Desjardins at all. What controls were put in place? How did the rogue employee conduct their nefarious business without detection? That's where the focus needs to be.

Similarly, a Capital One financial data breach was tied to the detection of "an outside individual" who was able to get unauthorized access to personal information from Capital One credit card customers. That person was arrested. Case closed. But the case isn't closed. It's barely open. They wanted to satisfy their outcome bias. The criminal was arrested and, we assume, will be convicted and sentenced, and that's where the investigation started and ended.

The physicist Richard Feynman, when he was young and working on the atomic bomb at Los Alamos in the New Mexican desert in the 1940s, had a habit of, well, safe-cracking. He was bored in those confined circumstances and would take it upon himself to open any lock he could. As he later wrote, "To demonstrate that the locks meant nothing, whenever I wanted somebody's report and they weren't around, I'd just go in their office, open the filing cabinet, and take it out. When I was finished I would give it back to the guy: 'Thanks for your report.'

""'Where'd you get it?'

"'Out of your filing cabinet.'

"'But I locked it!'

"'I know you locked it. The locks are no good.'"[3]

People changed their locks. In fact, they changed their safes. But Feynman kept coming for them: "I opened the safes which contained all the secrets to the atomic bomb: the schedules for the production of the plutonium, the purification procedures, how much material is needed, how the bomb works, how the neutrons are generated, what the design is, the dimensions—the entire information that was known at Los Alamos: the whole schmeer!"

Because we want justice to win out, we conveniently avoid looking at the bigger picture, the one in which the puzzle of figuring out how to open a lock just means that Feynman, and hackers, will try even harder to crack it. This means that the real issues, the disconnects between the incentive to hack and the ability to stop a hack, haven't been addressed. Terminating an employee or vendor, or arresting an outsider, only provides a short-term reward, but creates longer-term headaches. Terminating a business contract that bound the vendor to the client, for example, only starts to place both companies' focus on their legal liability, which makes them less open and cooperative when it comes to the investigation. In fact, a study of 650 security and IT professionals indicated that 44 percent of their companies experienced a material breach at the hands of their vendors, and about 49 percent terminated the contract.[4] It's the "Ready. Shoot. Aim." approach.

We have to set aside our biases, worry less about getting back at the culprit, and focus more on protecting our businesses and ensuring a future repeat of the breach doesn't occur.

So, how do we avoid these biases and get to the root causes? How do we learn from our mistakes instead of continually repeating them?

We can learn from the airline industry. In the United States, the National Transportation Safety Board investigates incidents and makes recommendations that the Federal Aviation Authority then mandates throughout the industry, creating an ever-improving cycle of airline safety. Perhaps because of the nature of airline safety, and the fact that we are afraid for human lives, we, as a society, demand this process.

We need to do the same when it comes to cybersecurity. Data breaches present ubiquitous and destructive financial and personal consequences for individuals and for organizations. Although security experts and employees don't have to worry about calculating fuel loads in both imperial and metric, they are beholden to data privacy laws and regulatory requirements for breach reporting. The continuous improvement of compliance practices and resulting protection of consumer rights and privacy needs to be a priority. Will we ever get to the point where we conduct public inquiries into major security events? Unfortunately, there are a lot of barriers. First, no company wants its shortcomings spelled out through a public investigation. Lawyers will fight to ensure such liability-creating issues are not exposed to the light of day. It will take government to legislate and mandate such investigations beyond what the Office of Civil Rights does today.

In early 2018, the SEC updated their regulations to bring the boardroom into the conversation. Following the Equifax breach in which several executives ultimately pleaded guilty to selling stock knowing that the company was about to announce a massive data breach, the SEC created guidelines that define how funds disclose cybersecurity risks to investors, new rules to create a blackout trading window following the discovery of a cybersecurity event to prevent insider trading. Even looking at this breach, however, where the findings from their inquiry provide specific measures that the Federal Trade Commission mandated the company to adopt, the required changes don't account for new trends and correlated issues needed to create standards for companies to follow and for consumers to use as a guide to their rights.

Even the New York financial institutions governed by the Department of Financial Services (DFS) got into the act and pulled similar credit management organizations under their auspices. The DFS cybersecurity rules and regulations (NYCRR 500) represented the gold standard of breach reporting, with companies required to report a material cyber breach within seventy-two hours.[5] Moreover, under the DFS, firms would have to contribute to an annual declaration on the part of the client in which not only material breaches are inventoried, but unsuccessful attempts are also documented. This can be a significant task for banks with large security teams, let alone a small law firm outsourcing IT operations.

In 2018, global privacy and data breach laws took control across Europe in the form of the General Data Protection Regulation (GDPR), and in 2019, Canada introduced the Canadian Breach of Security Safeguards Regulations of the Personal Information Protection and Electronic Documents Act (PIPEDA). In the United States, 2020 sees the activation of the California Consumer Privacy Act. Each set of regulations and laws continues to define how businesses collect and use consumer data, and their obligations to protect this data from misuse, theft, or exposure to unauthorized parties.

But change will take a long time. And, given that these breaches affect hundreds of millions of consumers, it's hard to imagine what magnitude will overcome our lethargy and tendency to continue accepting these breaches and the financial consequences that are inflicted.

So, what happened to the 767?

Ah, yes, the 767 at the heart of our story. We left it plummeting over the middle of the Canadian prairies.

And it's here that we learn that human error can become human ingenuity.

Remember, it was a next-generation aircraft that introduced the industry to the concept of a digital cockpit, virtual operating controls, and computerized navigation. And like most new technology, it was less well understood by operators, and often glitchy. But with only a radio and some basic analog standby instruments, the pilots were metaphorically and literally left in the dark.

It was at that moment that Air Canada Flight 143 became a $40 million glider.

Captain Pearson was an experienced glider pilot and comfortable with powerless flight, understanding the value of altitude and speed. The higher and faster you are gliding, the farther you can go. It's the same principle as a paper airplane. Throw it from standing on the ground, and it travels a shorter distance than if you throw it from a second-story window.

First Officer Quintal rapidly calculated that they could not reach their alternate landing site in Winnipeg. Having previously served as a pilot in the Royal Canadian Air Force, Quintal knew of a disused air force base just north of their current position and suggested landing at this much closer safe haven. Trusting his copilot, Pearson turned the powerless 767 north towards Gimli, a small town on the shores of Lake Winnipeg. The flight crew lined up to make a dead-stick landing on runway 32L.

Unbeknownst to Pearson, Quintal, and the helpless air traffic controllers, the intended runway now served the Winnipeg Sports Car Club, as a multifunction auto racing facility. Much of the 6,800-foot runway had a steel guardrail running down the middle of it to create a two-lane dragstrip. The day of the incident, the racing club was hosting a family event with cars racing on the now decommissioned runway. Go-karts were racing on 32L past the drag strip portion of the runway. Race cars and campers surrounded the runway, as children and families enjoyed their festivities on a beautiful summer day. On the ground, air traffic controllers in Winnipeg frantically searched for alternate landing sites, but none of these sites were equipped with the emergency services surely needed in the aftermath of an emergency landing. They had to land on the dragstrip.

Without power, the flight crew lowered the landing gear, relying on gravity to lock it in place. Six nautical miles from touchdown, Pearson's experience and intuition told him the aircraft was too high and traveling too fast to safely land without sliding off the end of the runway. Pearson threw the plane into a forward slip, effectively snowplowing the plane sideways through the air, which increases drag, slows the plane, and rapidly loses altitude. It's a common maneuver in light aircraft and gliders but was unheard of in commercial airliners. Several hundred feet from the ground, passengers on the left side of the plane stared at the sky, while the passengers on the right side of the cabin could count the trees and see the faces of the golfers below. One terrified passenger later remarked, "I could almost see what club they were using."

Captain Pearson waited until the very last moment to straighten out the aircraft just before touchdown, and in the final seconds, Pearson saw two boys riding their bicycles right where the plane was going to touch down. And with both engines out, the plane made virtually no noise as it approached. Luckily, one boy looked back at his friend and spotted the plane, and Pearson later remarked that he could see the terror on the child's face. As the plane touched down, the unlocked front landing gear predictably collapsed, smashing the nose of the 767 into the runway. Remarkably, the plane straddled the guardrail as the nose slid along the ground. Their potential nemesis became an ally and prevented the out-of-control plane from careening off the runway and into the families and children watching the crash landing unfold.

Seventeen minutes after running out of fuel, Air Canada Flight 143 came to final rest, mere yards from the racing cars and the event's participants. All crew and passengers were safe. The families on the ground were spared a horrific tragedy. Because the plane came to rest in a 140-tonne downward dog with its tail in the air, ten passengers were injured using the rear emergency evacuation slides, which sat at too steep an incline for safe use. The sixty-one passengers, eight crew members, and hundreds of people attending the event survived. Media subsequently nicknamed the flight "the Gimli Glider." Subsequent attempts by multiple flight crews in 767 flight simulators ended in major crashes that would have resulted in catastrophic loss of life.

Although the pilot and copilot were hailed as heroes, the airline's investigators determined that insufficient fuel was loaded into the plane for the scheduled flight and faulted the flight crew, which resulted in a demotion for Captain Pearson and suspension for First Officer Quintal. The three ground crew maintenance workers involved were also suspended. But, following an appeal, the air crew were returned to operational status. Captain Pearson flew for another ten years for Air Canada and retired from his aviation career in 1995. Years later, Quintal was promoted to captain, and at the age of sixty-eight, died in his Quebec hometown.

Pearson's sheer piloting skills avoided a total tragedy.

Companies get taken down by criminals, inside and out, because they're not paying attention to what really matters. Our biases hinder how we respond to crises. Human error is often targeted as the cause of incidents. But by chalking it up solely to this, we stop investigating other factors around the human at the center of it—such as the environment, policies, employee training, security controls, social requirements, political and workplace pressures, budget and resourcing decisions: the systemic factors that aim big but sometimes prevent us from doing our best.

Our biases hinder how we respond, but like Captain Pearson, we often have the tools that we need to glide to a safe place. We can't stop investigating all of the factors around the human at the center of the action, and we have to begin to build expertise so that we can prevent unwanted outcomes even when we've miscalculated our security tactics, and so we can adapt in an ever-evolving world. Business will be digital-world dominated by nebulous perimeters, distributed workforces, global connections, decision-making driven by artificial intelligence, and critical systems moving to the public cloud. These changes are only going to increase in speed and complexity.

There are no safe spaces, as we'll discuss in the next chapter. But there is safety in numbers, and we can count on each other.

5

NO SAFE SPACES

THERE'S A NEW presidential candidate up on the stage, forty thousand in the audience cheering her on. She's the one to beat. She's surrounded by dozens of military guards, her husband and children off to the side, beaming as she climbs the podium to gear up the crowd. Her message is positive. She's young, only in her early forties, and the atmosphere is electric, people raising up their phones to take her picture and post on social media. She smiles and waves, then adjusts the microphone as she starts her speech. Mid-sentence, she stops as her eyes widen, and her body shakes as if she's been hit by the fifty thousand volts of the electrodes of a Taser pulse. She falls down.

The Secret Service agents look around and see nothing. No Taser, no gun. Everyone in attendance has gone through a body scan before getting in the door. No one is running away. There's a hush through the crowd as she's quickly lifted up and out to a waiting ambulance.

Her husband is pointing the paramedics to her MedicAlert bracelet. The candidate was born with a hole in her heart, and she has an implanted pacemaker. But just as the paramedics settle her and get her breathing steady, she starts shaking again. The pacemaker is shocking her heart, and there's nothing they can do to stop it. They're rushing her to hospital but they can't do anything: the shocks are coming over and over again, so much so that her body is overwhelmed and surrenders to the crazed assault by the implanted device designed to save her life. No one can save her. Her candidacy, her future, her life, it's all gone.

Investigators find out that there was no health issue that would have predicated her heart going into shock. The pacemaker didn't malfunction, either. It was instructed to shock her, repeatedly, to kill her. Once a hacker was able to tap into her implanted device, the candidate no longer had control over her own fate. She could be destroyed from the inside out, from three hundred feet away through the power of a simple smartphone, and no one would ever know the better. Anyone could be taken down in an instant; not just this candidate, but anyone, famous, infamous, or neighbor down the street, if they had to rely on a medical device like this one.

This never happened. But it could. In fact, in 2013, Vice President Dick Cheney revealed that in 2007, manufacturers disabled the wireless feature in his implanted defibrillator to prevent a hacker from doing exactly what was described in the story above. And it's not fiction. Art does imitate reality.

In 2019, the FDA issued a warning alerting both patients and health care providers to the presence of security vulnerabilities in devices produced by the company Medtronic. Designing and building implantable devices such as insulin pumps and various models of cardiac implants, Medtronic is one of the largest medical device companies in the world. But only a year earlier, the company had already disabled its pacemaker programmer updates for 34,000 devices because of security issues. Now, Medtronic's entire operations process had to be shut down in order to recall most of their new implantable products. CareLink, the internal software used by Medtronic, didn't have a satisfactory security protocol in place. It turns out that it was just too easy for someone other than the patient to access the pump and change its settings.

During the COVID-19 outbreak, the most heinous attacks targeted overworked health care workers. Fake emails supposedly sent from their IT teams with the subject "ALL STAFF: CORONAVIRUS AWARENESS" informed employees that "the institution is currently organizing a seminar for all staff to talk about this deadly virus" and solicited employees to click on a link to register.[1] In one case, a Czech hospital was shuttered after a coronavirus-themed attack.[2]

Preparing for the worst means thinking like criminals, not like IT specialists. Recently, researchers in Israel announced that they created a computer virus capable of adding tumors into CT and MRI scans designed to fool doctors into misdiagnosing high-profile patients. Likewise, a computer technology–enabled intravenous pump could say that it was pushing the required dosage, yet actually inject enough drugs to kill a person in minutes. The intentional misrepresentation of medical information can not only lead to misdiagnoses, it can lead to international political issues, social strife, and legal minefields. Hospitals are primed for hackers taking advantage of any opportunity to insert an operational disruption that will expedite a ransom being paid.

But let's not get ahead of ourselves. These are extreme challenges that require a new mindset, and a new level of creativity to predict the worst of what is to come. Ransomware attacks on health care, and the loss of associated data, will cost global health organizations nearly $6 trillion in damages this year, compared to $3 trillion in 2017. The reality is, however, that we need that same new mindset to solve smaller, everyday issues in hospitals and care centers around the world.

Researchers at Vanderbilt University compared the U.S. Department of Health and Human Services' list of health care breaches with patient mortality rates at more than three thousand hospitals. Of the 10 percent that had suffered cyberattacks, patient care increased by 2.7 minutes.[3] What does this mean? It took an average of 2.7 minutes more for hospital staff to figure out what was wrong with a patient, and to help them. That 2.7 minutes mattered. We've all seen on television shows, or even experienced in real life, what a team of medical personnel has to do in a matter of moments when someone is having a heart attack or bleeding out. This 2.7 minutes led to as many as thirty-six cybersecurity-related deaths per ten thousand patients.

Ransomware kills.

It's getting harder to protect hospitals and patients

In the middle of a snowstorm at one of the busiest health care centers on the outskirts of Indianapolis in January 2018, Hancock Regional Hospital administrator Steve Long received a phone call from his systems administrator. It was the middle of flu season, and the hospital was full, but Long had to shut down every computer and system immediately while he dealt with a forward plan. In a hospital, that doesn't just mean office computers. Patient monitors, radio-frequency identification (RFID) technology, and machines responsible for managing dialysis, those helping patients breathe, and those keeping track of the very heartbeats of the most vulnerable surgery survivors often have to be turned off during such an attack. Everything is integrated. Like other high-risk industries such as banking, flight management, and traffic control, health care systems keep track not only of people and their needs but of the medical technology systems hospitals use to keep people alive.

The hospital leadership team at Hancock was expecting something like this. In interviews with the press, Long suggested that he was fully aware of the risk, and the immediate demand for a cryptocurrency transfer, that many of his colleagues in the health care field had been aiming to protect themselves from recently. The 2017 WannaCry ransomware attack had wormed its way through 230,000 computers in over 150 countries, including those in major health systems in the United States and the United Kingdom in particular. If they aren't prepared, U.S. organizations can be fined under HIPAA (Health Insurance Portability and Accountability Act of 1996) for exposing personal patient data.

Think about all of the medical technologies that are linked to computer systems. The biggest vulnerability in a hospital is the requirement for access, and that means timely access, to patient records, to systems that provide life-giving emergency support, and to medical images. Simple things like terminals, medical imaging systems like X-rays and CT scans—all of these are connected to the network. If these systems are not technologically segmented properly, and are hacked, criminals can move laterally through these simple tools to somewhere else in the network. A hacker may sit in the waiting room, ostensibly waiting for a friend getting an MRI scan, and from that location hack into a workstation that can provide a gateway right to the CEO's office or to central patient records. We also now have electronic medical records systems that can integrate the use of many different devices with radio-frequency capabilities, such as insulin pumps and other drug delivery systems, heart rate monitors, and pacemakers. Wearable and implantable devices like these are now standard tools in 60 percent of U.S. hospitals. Hospitals even have the ability to monitor people's movements, including the amount of time and distance they walk and run, as well as to operate home-sleep monitoring systems from a distance.

According to field research, devices that transport medical data are not secure because the memory of the devices is limited; authentication and secure communications protocols are required to protect the data and the device. Nonetheless, the greatest threat to mobile devices of any kind comes from malware that can become embedded in applications, and the fact that these are always connected to a network. Mobile application development in health care has exploded, but the capability of sending mobile malware to devices has also exploded at the same time. Malware has infected wireless-enabled devices and is capable of propagating itself to other devices.

What do hackers want from hospitals and other organizations? Generally, we're talking about four major areas of interest in patient health care records:

1   To encrypt or steal large-scale or individual personal data, and hold the data for ransom, assuming a near-immediate return.

2   To resell large-scale personal data for a delayed, but larger return.

3   To phish individuals exposed in the large-scale personal data pool for a delayed, but larger return.

4   To find some specific individual data, with the intention of selling the information, sometimes including specific profiles or names, to third parties, or of using it for a personal threat or another crime. This is akin to whale phishing (going after highly lucrative individuals).

Another trend is appearing. Beyond ransoming patient records, criminals are using the same malware to cripple hospital operations. This critical service disruption allows criminals to extort the hospital for larger sums, which means that we're talking about hackers making money on both sides of the same criminal coin.

Why are these technologies linked to radio-frequency systems? Machine-to-machine devices, many of which include RFID technology, are made of inexpensive sensors that are deployed across many different domains in order to manage our lives. When it comes to health care, that means that doctors and nurses can, ostensibly, keep track of high-risk patients, such as the elderly, frail, and those with complex medical conditions, at home. They can monitor their medications and their vital signs. Health care professionals can check in and, at a distance, up a dose or ensure that an ambulance is on the way.

The same is true for other IoT-connected devices. Smart power grids, car telematics, and digital home networks are linked. Mobile devices, such as smartphones, tablets, sensors, and laptop computers, have become tools for everyday life. Our books, televisions, bikes, cars, and homes are wired to ensure that we can move information quickly, when we want to, to order groceries from our fridges and call up a soundtrack to our lives on our speaker systems. The problem is that the way devices are used may jeopardize our safety and personal privacy. We don't choose great passwords. We skip software updates. And all of our mobile devices are full of sensitive information about users and the companies that employ them; this vital intelligence on users can be used to gain access to internal business and personal networks and systems. Mobile devices are no longer just targets for low-level hackers, but are now sought out by criminals seeking to steal personal and business communications and data by burrowing into networks the easy way.

When connected technology can kill

A few years ago, a presentation was scheduled at the Black Hat conference in Las Vegas. Barnaby Jack, an expert in the field of embedded device security, was going to demonstrate to the world just how easy it would be to hack into a medical RFID device. Within a fifty-foot radius, he had revealed in previous presentations, he could send an electric shock of up to 830 volts to the heart of anyone using an implanted pacemaker. Within three hundred feet, he could reach any insulin pump embedded in a human body and put it into overdrive. He didn't need these medical parts' identification numbers or RFID tags.[4] He could simply broadly hack into the radio frequency and deliver a heart attack or a hypoglycemic shock, either of which could instantly kill a patient. If someone's pancreas, heart, kidneys, lungs, or blood pressure was tapped into a system aimed at keeping them alive, Jack illustrated to the health care field, it was theoretically possible to take their life at a distance. Before he could reveal his next secrets, however, Jack's girlfriend found him dead in his apartment. The coroner ruled the cause of his death a drug overdose.

The lessons he taught the health care community didn't go unheeded.

Hancock Regional Hospital was one of the many organizations that stepped up their cybersecurity efforts, knowing that these possibilities existed. The problem was that they also missed something critical along the way. Although the hospital had implemented the most strategic, expensive, and technologically sound security system they could afford, they still got hacked. Cybercriminals accessed the credentials of a vendor that sold hardware for one of the information systems used by Hancock. In other words, in protecting themselves, the hospital created a liability.

And what did the hackers want? In this case, the ransom was a measly four Bitcoin, at the time worth roughly $55,000. That's it. But the hospital's systems were offline for more than twenty-four hours, requiring critical patients to be moved to other health care centers and Hancock's entire IT systems to be scrubbed.

Not just big businesses are on the hook

Cybercrime affects some of the most hardworking people-oriented organizations out there, and we're starting to learn why that is the case. Hancock, like other hospitals, is vulnerable because their focus is often required elsewhere. This means that they aren't immune to attack even if their revenues aren't as free flowing as Wall Street's and the money on the line is minimal. Operational disruption in these cases could lead to death, and speculations about cybersecurity holes in an RFID-ready world suggest that we need to move faster at protecting our health care systems during future natural disasters and pandemics like COVID-19.

Think about the day-to-day operations at an average health care unit. Things move fast as people are triaged, and care is hands-on. Machines can be employed for tests or for emergency support, but beyond check-in, health care workers don't usually stop to enter data every moment of the day. In other words, people aren't staring at a screen in medical industry culture; they're staring at their patients' bodies, looking for clues. And let's not forget the physical nature of hospitals: they're open. In a private corporation, people have to pass through all sorts of controls to get into building. In a hospital, the doors are unlocked. People are running. The nature of the business is time sensitive. You can't have mass restrictions on systems or even data in place, because signature approvals aren't going to take place when patients are about to die on the operating table.

Compounding the issue is the fact that the vast majority of hospitals don't have full-time IT employees in place. This is especially true in the countries where IT teams are shared across hospitals and medical care organizations. In other words, to do their business, hospitals must have systems, but visibility and vigilance over those systems are hard to achieve given their priorities. The same is true for hospital computers and the data records that they keep. A lot of medical systems also, unfortunately, operate on old legacy operating systems like Windows XP, for example, because the budget priorities lie elsewhere. XP is not supported anymore, and it was a leaky sieve even when it was supported more than a decade ago. When there's an older computer in the mix, few updates take place. Medical staff are trained in privacy compliance, and they know their obligations around patient records, but their security training can be limited, or they view security as directly in conflict with their focus on patient treatment priorities.

But some of the same issues crop up even when a hospital is very well funded. The fact is that everybody looks at security through its potential for return on investment: is spending money on security going to make us money, or cost us money? Many hospitals in the United States, for example, have parent organizations that centralize and harmonize services and staff. With a corporate approach to health care, we know that revenue is generated by physicians and medical care, beds, and medical equipment. The more patients who are helped through each hospital, whether private or public, the more money is generated.

But that isn't the real issue at stake.

Even setting aside the ethical reason for security of protecting human lives (which, let's be real, ought to be the only consideration), what is the cost of violating HIPAA regulations? What is the cost of the hundreds or thousands of lawsuits that a U.S. hospital will undergo if they put patient lives at risks or, through a malware attack, share private medical data with hackers?

And let's not forget that hospitals have the same issue that other businesses have. HIPAA interviewed health care workers at different hospitals across the United States and found that attacks on the C-suite are twelve times more likely than on other employees, and C-suite execs are nine times more likely to be the target of social incidents.[5] Hospital leaders need to take the same vigilance with security as they take to protecting patient privacy under HIPAA and other national laws. They have to pay attention, and they need to stop the gaps in their many-years-long purchasing cycles for new computers and systems that can do much of the work for them.

Creating safe spaces

Hospitals that are on top of this issue are practicing for the eventuality that they will face down a hacker at some point. Take the example of a patient who is having a stroke, Nicole Wetsman writes in *The Verge*,[6] and who needs an emergency CT scan, only to have his caregivers see a flash for a Bitcoin payment request threatening to shut down the devices needed to supply the right solution to that patient before the stroke overwhelms him. Maricopa Medical Center in Arizona has been running through these scenarios with their team on the regular, even though they've never experienced a breach.

Creating safe spaces, however, isn't just a matter of running through worst-case scenarios. No matter what kind of organization is at stake, security challenges can be broken down into four layers: data collection, communications, computing, and action. Where are your policies, your controls of people, processes, and technologies, and your analyses of risk falling short? Do you have existing methods to test compliance against the framework in which you're operating? What are your acceptable alternatives if everything fails?

Challenges within each of these layers can include deployment, maintenance, and measurements as well as the risk of failure, especially in an RFID environment, because of the complexity and number of hard-to-manage devices. The vast number of devices being deployed runs the risk of overwhelming the wireless communication networks and threatens the security and privacy of the ecosystem. Let's not forget, as the FDA has warned us, that standards are still under development and that existing solutions are fragmented. Solutions are being designed from scratch, but conventional IT design standards lack policy and trust and do not address the challenges in the organizational ecosystem, and many of our newest tools lack the proper data analytics, data security, and sensor management needed.

Put it like this. Regulators had strong controls to warn of the risk of electrical shock from inserting a metal utensil into a plugged-in toaster. But there are no brightly colored stickers to warn consumers that the toaster might be used to steal money from their smart-connected countertop appliance.

Different network protocols, data formats, incompatible devices, and multiple applications lead to major security and privacy concerns, and this is especially the case in hospitals, where many different systems have often been cobbled together, because it's too difficult, if not impossible, to create one synthetic data solution. As well, security and privacy controls for mobile devices are created by mobile application developers, network systems engineers, and security architects, but these are likely to rely on lessons learned from decades of desktop protection policies. This approach leads to only a partial view of the entire attack and requires great human effort to configure and deploy applications.

What can you do to create a digital safe space?

- Have you created an air gap between critical systems and publicly accessible networks?

- Have you managed just-in-time administrative access through two-stage approvals?

- Have you used device management tools to control the access to critical devices such as IV pumps?

- Have you applied the least privilege principle with zero administrative controls for medical staff?

- Have you completed thorough testing of devices to not only validate clinical efficacy but to test backdoor access through firmware or IP networks?

The potentially critical nature of health care and the potential threats to human safety mean that security must take a higher priority than in the past. It's our job as a society to ensure that we do everything we can not to endanger human life. HIPAA knows it. The FDA knows it. And they're holding all of us accountable.

6

ALL THE PLANS IN THE WORLD

"**WE HAVE EVERYTHING** they ever created," The Dark Overlord boasted to *Vice* magazine's online cyber news site, Motherboard, in 2016 through their online chat service. "We approached them with a handsome business proposition. However, there has been a moderate dispute."[1]

The Dark Overlord, which we'll get to in a few moments, was talking about hacking into Gorilla Glue, one of the largest private manufacturing organizations in the United States, based in Sharonville, Ohio. We all know Gorilla Glue from strolling the aisles at Home Depot and Lowe's: their bright orange labels stand out, and they make things stick together better than any other company in the market. But they're a little different than most big businesses, in that Gorilla Glue is family-owned and operated. They're a big deal but they act like they're not, with a let's-do-this-the-fun-way orientation where every employee is in on the joke.

What The Dark Overlord told Motherboard was simple. They wanted to extort Gorilla Glue, and since the company wasn't paying up, Motherboard was supposed to interpret the message so that it would become clear to the decision-makers involved. The Dark Overlord had co-opted insider information on Gorilla Glue, enough of it that, should they release it, the magic glue formula would be public knowledge. The hackers claimed that they had over five hundred gigabytes of the company's intellectual property: research and development information, product designs, credentials, and core infrastructure information like financial spreadsheets, invoices, strategic documents, presentations, contracts, and other internal material. To prove it, the hackers sent Motherboard a sample: two hundred megabytes of the cache files that they had lifted from Gorilla Glue's offices. Instead of locking up Gorilla Glue's files, they had effectively stolen them and threatened to bring down the company.

And it got worse. Not only did The Dark Overlord attack the company, they went right for the jugular. They started to send Motherboard photographs of Gorilla Glue's executives, employees, and their family members, something that the journalists were able to verify. They knew what they were doing. Blackmail is a well-established script to follow: seize information, and once you have access to it, make sure the vulnerable parties—in this case, a company and its individual leaders—know that they are at risk.

And if the recipient doesn't pay, what happens next?

Let's think about that for a second. Since Gorilla Glue is a private company, they chose not to share what was happening with Motherboard or any other members of the press. But what we have to assume is that they were frightened, especially as those photographs started leaking. The Dark Overlord had used personal information many times before and would do so many times after this event. *The Daily Beast,* for example, reported in late 2017 that members of The Dark Overlord sent texts to parents in Iowa threatening to kill their children.[2]

The Dark Overlord is also known as the Professional Adversarial Threat Group. It's not a single human who thinks he's in charge, but rather a group of hackers who operate extortion schemes that run the gamut from infantile to extremely dangerous. Like other hacking teams, it's a loose connection of people who are determined to get one over on anyone in their line of sight. Sometimes The Dark Overlord aimed to do nothing more than play with media schedules, releasing nine episodes of *Orange Is the New Black* and *New Girl* and a few other television shows in 2017 before they were scheduled to air. In other cases, they tried to play in the big leagues, hacking what came to be known as the 9/11 Papers—insurance files connected to the 9/11 attacks—from Lloyd's of London and Silverstein Properties. The suggestion made by The Dark Overlord was that, like the disclosures made by WikiLeaks, the revelation of these papers would change the way that we think about 9/11. The thing is, none of these efforts resulted in a huge exchange of money: as of 2019, only 1 percent of the ransom demands had been paid, and even the slow leak of information still taking place has revealed absolutely nothing new.

Cybercrime is about feelings, not numbers

Extortion plays on human emotion. It's a weapon, just of a different kind than we're used to. We used to throw stones, and now we shoot bullets, but it's still the same principle. We use objects to harm our opponents or adversaries. But instead of inflicting pain with a rock or a bullet, we inflict fear. The victim is pushed down into the lowest levels of Abraham Maslow's hierarchy of needs.

What does that mean? The hierarchy of needs is like a pyramid. It states that a human being's primary needs (for food, shelter, and security) have to be met first: these are the foundation of our personal pyramids. Once we understand that we are safe, we then can spend time developing our higher functions in life, like creating a business or writing a book. People aim for peak experiences, at the top of the pyramid, linked to what Maslow called self-actualization. This is where we feel content with our level of achievement in life and alignment with our own values. When we're faced with extortion, however, we fall right back down to the bottom of the pyramid: How can I find safety and security? Should I pay? What will happen if I pay? Will I be out of money? Will I set myself up for future threats? Am I putting myself into legal jeopardy? Will I put my family at risk? Have I committed a crime by sending money to criminals?

Extortion makes people vulnerable in ways that they can't even conceive of until it happens to them.

Often, in business, we like to believe that what we do comes down to brass tacks. What we count. What we bring into the coffers after we send products out the door. What matters is money, revenues, profits, and any combination thereof. Emotion doesn't factor into it, and if it does, we should ignore it. Proudly. But that's not what psychologists say actually takes place in a business.

Long before I was a cybersecurity expert, I was a psychology student, and I worked at a psychology lab, assisting in animal behavior and neural psychology experiments. What I know, and what the research shows, is that people are incapable of separating out their emotions from their decisions—in fact, we need emotions to make decisions. Neural analysis shows that people who lose the ability to use their emotions, because of a serious brain injury or some forms of strokes, find it near impossible to make even the simplest decisions, like which cereal to eat in the morning. Similarly, in business, we trust our emotions, often referring to them as our gut instincts, to choose the right marketing campaign or which product to send down the line or which accountant to hire.

What kind of extortion are we really talking about?

Indirect extortion is connected with the use of ransomware. Ransomware is probably our biggest threat because it has become a go-to tool for cybercriminals. Holding someone ransom, in a cybercriminal sense, is when a hacker encrypts and thereby locks critical files and demands a ransom to unlock them. It's a simple enough business model, and that is why it's been so successful in recent years. Like kidnapping, being held ransom feels scary and heartbreaking. Once, and only when you have proof of life, you'll have to pay out to release a loved one or important business or political figure. In this case, it's an exchange of funds not to save a life but rather to arrange for the return of valuable data or access to your own files.

The cousin of ransom is **direct extortion**, otherwise known as blackmail. In this case, a person or company ends up paying to prevent the exposure of information to the public. If you could be in a compromising situation, someone will be able to exploit that.

At the end of 2019, LifeLabs in Canada was hacked. The company collects blood and other medical samples, as well as medical imaging like MRIs and X-rays, and their systems are directly connected to physicians' offices and hospitals, which both order these samples and receive the results. In this hack, the personal medical records of over fifteen million people were violated. While breaches of medical records are nothing new, this attack offers a unique opportunity beyond the simple resale of stolen records used in insurance scams. People's lives, behaviors, disorders, and treatments can be identified or inferred from these files.

Any one of these individual files could have a life-altering impact. In Harlan Coben's novel *The Stranger*, an unknown individual confronts people with irrefutable evidence of secrets kept by their loved ones that end up turning their lives upside down. In some cases, the stranger demands money to prevent the publication of these disastrous secrets.[3]

Like the protagonist in this book, LifeLabs's records contain information that many people don't want exposed. There are many levels of sensitivity in medical tests. Having a blood test to determine whether your liver and kidney can metabolize high blood pressure pills is common, and perhaps not a great reveal, but let's step it up a notch. What about someone sending your family and coworkers proof that you are taking medication to help with sexual dysfunction? It's not a life-threatening issue, but it is deeply personal and perhaps embarrassing. Let's go even further. What if your partner learns you are on medication for a sexually transmitted disease or a terminal illness that you've not yet discussed? Now we're wandering into an ethical minefield.

Consider what would happen if a hacker, or someone who bought data from hackers, sent your employer evidence that you are taking medication to treat a drug or alcohol addiction? Or that you are on antidepressants or antipsychotics? Not all employers would act ethically. Criminals could use blackmail to extort you so that they won't release this information to anyone (and there is never a guarantee), based on the fact that you fear that it might see the light of day. Even if no one cared about your medical history, your own fear could make them successful.

A story of leaked fertility records, even though not a story of extortion, demonstrates how damaging this information can be. In 2017, a woman in treatment for in vitro fertilization accidently discovered her own medical records while googling information about medical pregnancy assistance. It turns out that her private health care facility in the United Kingdom,

Lister Hospital, was routinely transferring unencrypted records by email to a company in India for transcription. They'd been doing it for nearly ten years. That organization did not protect the patient data, and it was picked up by web crawlers and made public through organic search. The U.K.'s Information Commissioner's Office fined the organization £200,000 for the infraction. But that fine did nothing to reverse time and protect this poor woman from exposing her deeply personal medical procedure.

When we are subject to extortion, those vulnerabilities become obvious. It feels painful because it *is* painful to see our hard work jeopardized by a random stranger. It feels like a violation because our work is emotional to us, and it matters to us to do well and to feel as if we are leading the way. We can't get around the emotional part of it. And so, we have to look at the hard facts: a lack of risk management also makes people vulnerable because it hits us where we live.

More risk means more planning

Creating a risk management plan is about creating a different kind of foundation, one that is tied to your cybersecurity ideology and ultimately about ensuring that you are never vulnerable to extortion of any kind. What plan did Gorilla Glue have in place for an incident response to a threat of this magnitude? We don't know. But I know what I would have done if I were in their position.

Imagine yourself sitting across a table from a mobster who has asked you to negotiate and has poured you a glass of wine to loosen you up. The mobster says, "I want you to pay me money," and pushes an envelope across the table, an envelope that he says holds pictures that he thinks could get you in trouble.

Step one is to verify that he actually has something of value. It's possible that the envelope is a collection of random pieces of paper of no value whatsoever. So you look: Are the contents of the envelope what he says they are? And will they cause you trouble if revealed?

Step two is to walk away from the table, leaving that glass of wine, and call the police or a friend for advice. Should you take the deal? What's going to make you the safest?

In the case of The Dark Overlord, the same rules apply.

Start with step one. If they have what they say they have on your company, is it really a loss if they reveal it to the world? And let's back up a moment here and get to the real issue: should the secret sauce for your product be sitting on an open server, ever? In fact, through what the industry calls the fourth industrial revolution, pan-connected manufacturing automation systems, called manufacturing execution systems (MES), contain recipes and control the cooking process. While these systems optimize manufacturing processes and offer the opportunity for big-data analytics to further streamline manufacturing, they present an easy portal to steal such information, or to sabotage by tweaking the recipe or changing elements of the assembly process.

Step two: do a risk assessment. In this case, call your general counsel and get some legal perspectives, and find out where and when you should get the police involved (probably right away). Now, honestly, is any law enforcement going to tell you to pay a ransom? No. But again, back up a moment. The risks posed by the exposure of literally every piece of information your company has, whether internal data and methods or external customer identities, or anything else, should have been assessed well before a hack ever takes place. And involving your general counsel invokes attorney-client privilege and protects potentially damaging information from being discoverable in future legal actions or court battles.

It seems so easy, correct? Plan ahead. Understand your risks. But the reality is that most businesses are not really looking at where their vulnerabilities lie.

That's why you're going to need a business continuity plan, a data recovery plan, a risk management plan, and an incident response plan in place if you're going to do cybersecurity right. But each plan has to be specific to your industry and your business. There's no one-size-fits-all approach. Managed detection and response scenarios have to match and align with your specific goals and needs if they are to going to be effective.

Let's take the case of a business email compromise (or BEC for short) hack that resulted in a U.S. defense contractor sending a group of cybercriminals $3.2 million worth of sensitive military gear that they weren't even supposed to know existed. Investigative reporters at *Quartz* got hold of legal documents filed by the anonymous "Company B," in Maryland, which suggest that they were hacked by a navy contracting officer who called himself Daniel Drunz and ordered up the gear to be sent to Los Angeles via a false purchase order. He also received $6.3 million worth of LG televisions and $1.1 million worth of Apple products along with the military equipment, no questions asked. Company B and the military only found out about the scam when a payment never arrived at Company B's door.[4]

Let's look at this case more carefully. When we're talking about over $10 million worth of product ordered up in a moment, who is authorized to make that transaction happen? Who gets on the telephone to confirm the transfer of equipment when the order is larger than normal or includes sensitive materials? Where is the check for secondary approval? How is it that a junior-level accounting person in a satellite office of an organization can make such a decision, rather than the CFO or, at the very least, a project manager or compliance officer?

We live in a world in which we have absolutely nothing left to lose. In the year before this book was published, a

Toyota subsidiary got caught up in a $37 million BEC scam. In another case, $11 million was hacked out of Caterpillar's U.K. office. Japanese cryptocurrency exchange Bitpoint lost about 3.5 billion yen ($32 million). And these stories are told over and over again. There's something wrong here. Right? Our corporate assumptions have a broken mechanism that says that we don't have a duty of care to engage in the best practices in risk management.

Let's go back to our story from the beginning of the chapter. The only legal repercussion of The Dark Overlord activities has been the late 2019 arrest of one of their members, Nathan Wyatt, who was previously caught stealing personal photographs from the iCloud account of Pippa Middleton, sister of Kate Middleton, Duchess of Cambridge. He's been extradited to the United States in connection with extortion charges that have yet to be fully revealed to the public. So, that's one person among possibly hundreds of members of The Dark Overlord.

We, not the computers, are the weakest link

Okay, so we can easily create firewalls and other risk management protocols on server-side software, through the use of middleware, and also in the design of sites and app software in order to protect people's identities and assets. We can physically stop hackers from accessing individual data sets that can help them to leach personal information, money, and password access. We need access control to data to create barriers, to prevent breaches and the possibility of phishing. We can also use computer network firewalls to assess risk, plug data holes, and prevent access without a password, and therefore to create pathways to the prevention, protection, and remediation of harm.

But cybersecurity is not a computer issue nor an IT problem to solve, as it is so often assumed. It's not about unpatched VPNs, as in the case of Travelex, or Apache servers like the Equifax breach. As I've been telling you, it's a business issue, and, even more than that, it is a people issue. Creating a data recovery plan is only a first step in the process. We know that cybersecurity risks are highest when a lack of care is given to how people communicate, connect, and process information. Making a commitment to changing the status quo on cybersecurity without taking a hard look at communication and team members' internal and external interactions at all levels of the organization is foolhardy.

Companies have to start with a risk inventory that is specific to their business and to their industry. Use asset liability management techniques. In other words, it's important to manage cybersecurity in the same way that you manage other assets: through constant risk management techniques that measure what matters, how it matters, and how it can be controlled. Ask yourself:

- What is confidential, proprietary, or protected in your business plan, in your assets and liabilities?

- What are your legal, regulatory, and customer privacy obligations towards those risks?

- What can you control and what is difficult to achieve right now?

- What is the gap between where you are now and where you'd like to be?

- How tolerant (or not) are you with each of these risks, and what would you do if a risk became a reality? Can you address this ahead of time?

Remember, exponentially growing risks are linked to new technologies such as AI or medical technologies, as we've discussed, and may not be addressed with a single annual probability assessment. How will you roll with changes over time, and who will be responsible for ownership of these challenges?

And, once you've thought about the risks, think about your business continuity plan.

- What happens when something goes wrong, and what are your first steps?

- What is your emergency incident response plan?

- Where's your backup?

- How are you creating training programs for employees to learn about how they can make informed choices in the case of an emergency?

Ultimately, it is always the unknown unknowns that impact performance in the face of a cybersecurity crisis, which means that true resilience comes from managing the unexpected. The essence and art of real cybersecurity is to do exactly that. But that's not how conventional approaches to security have been regularly understood and used in boardrooms in particular.

It's a leader's job to ask questions and build a company that understands security from the ground up. Businesses need to sort out the data management process itself from real security issues. This means that we may need a better planning model to build randomness into the process, taking into account real-life common sense and human experience, as well as the foibles of human nature. It can feel difficult to do this when IT experts speak an unfamiliar language. But a leader can bring the conversation back to risk, security performance, and corporate viability to shift the focus back to eliminating threats before they take hold.

We need clear and realistic thinking around what it takes to achieve these goals.

7

THE DOMINO EFFECT

O**N JANUARY 31, 2010,** a semi-submersible offshore drilling rig known as Deepwater Horizon arrived on the Macondo well to compete the exploratory drilling of Mississippi Canyon block 252 in the Gulf of Mexico. It's the closest drilling site to the Pass-a-Loutre State Wildlife Management Area in Louisiana, a 66,000-acre (270-km²) protected wetland in Plaquemines Parish that's known for fishing in its sediment-laden delta. But the rig was a safe bet. It was a $500 million unit built in 2001 in South Korea by Hyundai Heavy Industries, and the company leasing it, British oil giant BP, had been successfully using it for almost a decade through their operator, Transocean. Following exploratory drilling by another rig to verify prospecting results, the Deepwater Horizon took over to complete the drilling of the production well, before moving on from it in preparation for a production platform to extract the estimated 110 million barrels of hydrocarbons, namely oil or gas, from the reservoir.

Drilling for oil is a tenuous process because it's less of an exact science than we think. There's a lot of uncertainty compared with the past, where we were able to simply pull out gallons upon gallons with tiny pumps littering the hotter landscapes of the world. In the first place, oil companies have known for a long time that we're running out of sources. Although OPEC, which is responsible for the production of more than a third of the world's oil, has placed a focus on maintaining a surplus, the capacity of this surplus has dwindled in recent years, with production down to a third of what it was in the Middle East only a decade ago. And by the time Deepwater Horizon was moving through the gulf, oil in twenty-three Organisation for Economic Co-operation and Development inventories reached an average of sixty-eight million barrels, which amounts to only fifty-three days of oil reserves on a global basis. In other words, there wasn't much left in the pot. That's why, in the gulf and other places, new experimental protocols in geological exploration had come into play, including the use of radon mapping, seismic and structural mapping, integration of biological testing models, and computer simulation techniques that integrate multiple factors and models. And let's not forget about the money. The exploration side of the oil industry is also characterized as high-risk because of the sizeable investment level on the part of investors, as well as the range of geological, fiscal, and political uncertainties these investors need to bear both in their own locations as well as those associated with oil-producing countries. There is also risk associated with the sale of oil and gas products, related to uncertainty of the crude (supply) and the product market (offtake). Many oil- and gas-producing countries suffer from social and economic volatility, making them particularly prone to conflict and political instability.

Deepwater Horizon was built to address some of these risks. It holds the record for drilling the deepest well at 6.5 miles (10,500 m), which means that it was able to get at oil that had been sunk well below any previous expectations. Drilling low was also supposed to offset some of the environmental risk by keeping exploration well below human and most animal activity.

On the Macondo prospect, the rig was connected to a wellhead nearly five thousand feet below the surface of the gulf. By April 9, 2010, the Deepwater Horizon had drilled thirteen thousand feet into the Earth's crust. The total depth of that exploration was 18,360 feet (5,596 m). With the drilling complete, the next stage was to abandon the well. While the term "abandonment" might seem irresponsible or cavalier to the layman, it describes a routine operation to cap the well with a cement plug and conduct tests to ensure that no hydrocarbons can escape. To that end, on April 19, a special cement slurry, created by oil industry giant Halliburton, was pumped into the wellhead to form a seal. Initial tests indicated that well cap was holding. The following day, the crew of the Deepwater Horizon conducted two tests to verify initial findings. On the morning of April 20, the crew conducted what is known as a positive pressure test by applying 2,700 PSI of pressure to the wellhead seal assembly. This test again confirmed the well cap integrity, and the assembly was properly sealed. Later the same day, the second test began, leading to a massive gas leak, explosion, and sinking of the veteran rig.

Let's go a few hours back for a moment. In the early afternoon, the drill was run to a depth of over eight thousand feet in preparation for the second test, called the negative pressure test, to test all mechanical barriers. The test places the well in an underbalanced state where the pressure in the well is higher than the pressure in the drill pipe and a second control pipe, called the kill line. Mud in the well is displaced by pumping seawater into the well, and then the upper annular preventer (a large rubber doughnut that is mechanically squeezed against the opening) is closed to seal the well. Seawater is then pumped out, theoretically dropping the pressure in the drill pipe and upper assembly to zero PSI. Water continued to leak past the preventer, and the pressure on the annular was increased to 1,900 PSI in an attempt to stem the leak. With this stage complete, the well site leader ordered the negative pressure test to be run on the kill line (a feed used to control the pressure in the drill pipe) at 5:35 p.m. By 6:42 p.m., the drilling apparatus was reconfigured and a similar test was run on the kill line, with the pressure monitored for thirty minutes. No flow of seawater was detected (as expected), but the pressure in the drill line unexpectedly remained at 1,400 PSI.

Here's where it started to go wrong. The operations crew discussed this anomaly and concluded that the pressure was the result of a phenomenon called "the bladder effect," where pressure from the mud in the well is transmitted to the preventer and gives a false reading. Operators deemed the test complete at 8 p.m., and seawater was pumped out, and the pressure in the pipe was lower than the pressure in the reservoir.

That's when the pipe pressure increased to 100 PSI and the equivalent of thirty barrels of fluid pushed up through the pipe in less than ten minutes. This fluid was pumped overboard. By 9:31 p.m., three hundred barrels had flowed overboard and pressure had climbed to 550 PSI.

As the crew investigated the difference between the expected pressures and the measured pressure and fluid flow, mud overflowed onto the deck and shot up the vertical tower structure, called the derrick. At 9:40 p.m., the flow of mud was shunted to the mud-gas separator, where mud is diverted overboard and the gas is captured in a reservoir. Crews closed the annular preventer to stem the flow, but pressures rapidly increased to 1,200 PSI. Mud and gas spilled onto the deck of the rig. At 9:47 p.m., the first gas alarms sounded. Witnesses reported a roaring and vibration throughout the rig, and the pipe pressure rocketed to 5,700 PSI. A minute later, gas reached the air intake of the vessel's engines and the additional combustibles caused the engines to rev into overspeed.

At 9:49 p.m. electrical power was lost when two explosions occurred.

The second explosion caused extensive structural damage, including severing the control cables that connect the rig to the wellhead and communicate with the blowout preventer (BOP), a safety mechanism designed to automatically disconnect the rig from the wellhead. When communication is lost through these MUX cables, the fail-safe emergency disconnect system releases shears that crimp the pipe, automatically sealing the well. The BP report speculates that the loss of power might have resulted in the rig drifting off station, further damaging the drill pipe and BOP seal. The failure of the fail-safe systems resulted in a continued flow of gas.

At 9:52 p.m., when attempts to conduct an emergency disconnect failed, the order to abandon ship was given. Of the 126 crew members on board, 115 were rescued by helicopter and a nearby supply ship. Despite a three-day search and rescue operation by the U.S. Coast Guard, eleven crew were never found and were presumed dead. Nearly two days later, on April 22 at 10:21 a.m., the Deepwater Horizon sank, and uncontrolled release of hydrocarbons from the well resulted in the largest environmental disaster in the United States. It took multiple efforts to contain the uncontrolled flow from the well that spilled nearly five million barrels of oil (about 210 million U.S. gallons) and triggered unparalleled efforts to protect the gulf and Louisiana wildlife, wetlands, and economy from the adverse effects of the dispersed petroleum. The repercussions of the oil spill continue to filter through the U.S. economy a decade later by affecting tourism, food security, fishing and shrimping economies, amounting to a loss of $65 billion a year in revenue per coastal state estimated by authorities, with a total estimate of additional hidden costs to Louisiana and Mississippi of $61.41 billion. The devastation is likely far greater than one may assume.

What does this story have to do with cybersecurity?

The Deepwater Horizon story has *everything* to do with cybersecurity.

Deepwater Horizon was a risk management nightmare, and one that is very easy to understand because we all know about this story. We understand, on a gut level, what happens when crude oil hits water, and we've seen the news footage of the coastal devastation this disaster produced. Deepwater Horizon demonstrates, with relative simplicity, just how easy it is for something so well planned to go so wrong. Just like a cybersecurity event, this terrible incident illustrates exactly why something designed to be secure can be massively upended in an instant.

Let's look at why this event happened, and where the parallels lie between Deepwater Horizon and a cybersecurity event.

The findings of the BP investigation into the disaster isolated four contributing factors to the accident: (1) well cap integrity either was not established or failed; (2) hydrocarbons entered the well undetected and control of the well was lost; (3) the resulting escaped gases caused a crippling fire on the Deepwater Horizon; and (4) the blowout preventer did not seal the well. Each contributing factor had multiple factors that combined to cause serial failures leading to the disaster.

But what happened to put this domino effect into play? And how can we draw some connections here with the design of a cybersecurity risk management plan at any organization? There are four deeper factors to drill into.

DESIGN. First, on the Deepwater Horizon, a design flaw started the cascade of dominoes. As we'll see in detail below, the design of the cement cap contributed to the leak of hydrocarbons. If we're talking about cybersecurity risk, the parallel is failing to create an IT infrastructure that can resist most attacks and respond quickly to successful intrusions. This is basic. What systems can you install to make sure that your walls are up and your fortress is secure? Or at least, what defenses do you have to keep out the known threats?

SECURITY. Second, safety mechanisms failed to contain the flow of gas and prevent damage caused by the resulting fire. In cybersecurity, we're talking about a risk management plan predicated on preventing a security incident that goes undetected too long, metastasizes through the environment, and results in a massive data breach. If you start to notice something going wrong, or have the impression that you may be exposed in some way, can you shut down the hack or the leak fast enough? What's your plan?

HUBRIS. Third, operators assumed facts about test results that supported the desired outcome, and also took an hour and forty minutes to recognize the magnitude of the leak, gravely limiting their time to respond.

Assumptions can be a dangerous thing. Well beyond the adage about the word "assume" (which makes an "ass" of "u" and "me"), assumptions expose another bias. Much like the human biases we explored in chapter 4, this contributing factor to the explosion is a clear example of confirmation bias. That's our tendency to prefer data or interpretations that confirm or reinforce our belief system or a desired outcome.

In this case, BP executives and Transocean operators wanted the negative pressure test to report a sealed well, and so they interpreted the data to confirm that. When pressure in the riser didn't align to their expected result, they simply wrote the anomaly off as a result of an effect well-known in mining. It also meant that they were distracted and missed other signs that something was wrong. It cost the operators precious mitigation time to possibly avoid calamity. It also cost eleven of them their lives.

Here's where things feel more complicated, because we're talking about people and their assumptions. But, at the same time, both are easier to control than you might think. What's your compliance infrastructure? How have you trained your people in protecting the gates in the first place, and in responding to a possible crisis as it happens? Dwell time is everything. The faster an event is detected, the faster it can be contained. It's about cleaning up spilled milk rather than a nuclear meltdown.

COMMUNICATION. Fourth, a lack of communication between BP and their vendors introduced risks and errors in the abandonment process. Now, this is the hard part. Who is in charge, and who do they trust? We all know that, ultimately, we turn to a CEO or executive director when things go wrong. But, as we'll continue to unpack throughout these pages, those leaders often aren't in constant contact, strategically or operationally, with people on a company's IT team. There's a gap between these areas of management that can be exploited.

When a crisis occurs, blame is often placed on the people on the front lines, because everything feels like it should go back to design. But this isn't correct. The Deepwater Horizon story, as we will see in even greater depth below, highlights the fact that miscommunication, misunderstandings, and possibly misdirection across multiple organizations led to a catastrophic event.

In cybersecurity, this confluence of challenges is what we have to solve through what is called supply-chain or third-party risk management.

Miscommunication, missed notifications, and assumptions should all be controlled in contracts that govern how companies work together, what services are delivered, and roles and responsibilities. In cybersecurity terms, security incidents should be defined with clear triggers, reporting expectations, and timelines. Think GDPR or HIPAA in health care: there should be a maximum of seventy-two hours from initial discovery to initial notification. It's the golden rule.

Contracts should also cover roles and responsibilities when it comes to the installation and management of IT equipment. In one case, a hospital was compromised after a server was left unpatched and exposed to a well-known vulnerability. Why? Because the service provider was commissioned to install the equipment, not to maintain and patch it. But the hospital management assumed their systems were up to date. And they weren't—not because the service provider was incapable of it or didn't keep on top of the situation but because the hospital refused to pay an additional fee to cover ongoing maintenance. The hospital assumed that all that was necessary was to build the thing in the first place and didn't place value on taking care of it professionally.

What's the story behind the story?

Going back to Deepwater Horizon for a moment, it is important to recognize that BP, Transocean, and Halliburton were all operating under pressure to reduce costs by expediting the abandonment process. The operation was budgeted at $96 million, but at forty-three days over schedule, the costs had already ballooned to $150 million before the disaster took place. Industry expert Robert Bea, professor emeritus at the University of California, Berkeley and an investigator on the Deepwater Horizon, space shuttle *Columbia*, and *Exxon Valdez* disasters, commented that working with a $54 million overspend was like a "blowtorch on the bomb incentive: you can feel the heat and you are going to want to move fast."[1] Transocean blamed BP for cost pressures affecting the operation of the Deepwater Horizon.

So, in the midst of this bombshell moment, blame was making the rounds.

Given the depth of the well, as noted above, Halliburton had designed a special cement slurry that contained nitrogen gas to stabilize the cement and simplify the process of testing. Based on experience, however, Transocean employees objected to this approach, as it was shown to be unstable. Transocean alerted BP, suggesting that it would lead to a crisis event. BP overruled the objection. In its facilities in Louisiana, however, unbeknownst to BP or Transocean, Halliburton had run multiple lab tests and simulations and found nitrogen escaping from the slurry. Halliburton kept that information quiet.

The depth of the well also complicated the delivery of the cement. To ensure proper flow and distribution of the cement slurry, the feeder pipe must sit in the center of the drilling pipe. Given the five-thousand-foot length of the drilling pipe, Halliburton engineers recommended that they needed twenty-one centralizers to hold the feed pipe in place. There were only six centralizers on the Deepwater Horizon. Halliburton ordered fifteen more. The following day, BP canceled the order, citing different centralizer designs that risked a snag in the pipe. Email traffic between onshore engineers to offshore crew identifies the risk: "[The pipe] will not seek the perfect center of the hole unless it has something to centralize it. But who cares, its [sic] done, end of story. We'll probably be fine, and we'll get a good cement job."[2]

No mention of a blowout risk was communicated.

The story of the Deepwater Horizon and the subsequent investigations by the U.S. federal government, the U.S. Coast Guard, and BP exposed a chain of critical factors connecting flawed engineering designs, mechanical failures, suspect operational procedures, errors in human judgment, lack of contractor oversight, and miscommunication across multiple levels of the supply chain. Exploring this chain exposes lessons that apply equally to cybersecurity and data breach prevention.

The story behind the story is that we can avoid risks in one specific additional way, without systems, without protocols, and without checks and sign-offs: trust.

Human beings know what's wrong a lot of the time, but sometimes we don't give them the chance to speak out for fear of reprisal. The military takes what's called a "tactical pause" to assess rather than react. But outside the military, no one seems to want to take tactical pauses. Tactical pauses cause lost productivity or lost revenue. In business, we want to change the wheels on the race car and refuel the tank while it's driving at two hundred miles per hour and is leading the race. Pit stops are tactical pauses. We see this in the Deepwater Horizon disaster and we see this in every cybersecurity challenge: we feel pressured to work faster and to cut costs, and when people suggest that it might be better to slow down, to take a beat, and to listen to reason, they are often ignored or, worse, seen as a negative influence on a company that's simply pushing ahead to achieve higher revenues, higher profits, and influence in industry.

In many cases now, decisions about adopting new technology, like IoT, are made by business leaders and not by practitioners who understand the risks associated with untested technology. For example, in manufacturing, internet-connected systems are deployed by operational professionals like engineers who know everything about their assembly line and products, but little to nothing about IT security and how these connected devices are vulnerable to exploitation.

It happens inside and outside our companies as well. Our supply chain often becomes the overlooked or unwitting accomplice in security incidents and data breaches. We want them to cut costs; we want them to move faster as well.

Recently, I worked with a well-known research organization to interview 650 senior executives and security practitioners about their supply chain practices. We found that about a third of companies lack adequate resources to manage their supply chain partners, and two-thirds of the same companies didn't view vendor risk as a top priority. And that explains why nearly half of organizations have experienced a material breach as a result of their vendor's actions.[3]

Three stories jump to mind.

The first vendor breach that I'm thinking about are the attacks that took place on prominent Wall Street law firms Cravath, Swaine & Moore LLP and Weil, Gotshal & Manges LLP. These attacks demonstrated how stolen information from banks, investors, and technology firms could be used to front-run trades, a clear violation of SEC rules and federal market laws. In other words, criminals, in this case in the form of vendors, can break into law firms to find out private information about their clients: not to blackmail them or hold the data for ransom, but to create their own trading opportunities and get ahead of other investors.

The second example of a supply chain breach involves the compromise of a popular accounting software. MeDocs, part of many companies' supply chain, was weaponized and NotPetya ransomware was delivered to the user base on the Ukrainian accounting software from their hijacked FTP servers. NotPetya crippled the law firm DLA Piper, shipping firms, oil refineries, and hospital systems.

And the third supply chain breach involves a major trading firm, Tillage Commodities Fund. They filed a lawsuit that alleged that SS&C Technologies, their vendor, showed an egregious lack of diligence and care when they fell for an email scam that ultimately led to hackers in China looting $5.9 million from the fund.

What's worse than half of companies falling prey to vendor-caused security breaches is that, in our research, we found that only about 15 percent of vendors notified their customers of the breach. Putting it another way, 85 percent of businesses found out about the material breach when they discovered it themselves, or were notified by law enforcement or some equally disturbing source, rather than from their vendors or other partners in their supply chain. And it gets worse. Out of the organizations that were affected, seven out of ten made no post-breach changes to their vendor contracts, or to their management of the vendor.

Policies, prevention, and promises

When it comes down to it, this kind of behavior isn't business, it's gambling. We're gambling on a bet that it won't happen to us, this disaster, this cybersecurity crisis.

In doing so, in betting rather than planning, we're setting aside all of our stakeholder responsibilities. While the responsibility of a company to return a profit to shareholders must always be considered as part of its obligation, legally, there are many other stakeholders that need to be taken into consideration. To minimize harm and maximize benefit, companies have to build relationships of trust that involve becoming more transparent and open about the progress and setbacks that they experience and build a full-circle focus on trust in the workplace. We need to listen to each other in order to minimize the negative consequences of business activities and decisions on stakeholders, including employees, customers, communities, ecosystems, shareholders, and suppliers.

There are three kinds of approaches that can be taken to communicating with stakeholders. An **obstructionist approach** to stakeholder management is one that avoids corporate social responsibility; managers engage in unethical and illegal behavior that they try to hide from organizational stakeholders and society. In a more **defensive approach**, managers rely only on legally established rules to take the minimal position towards toeing the line. Finally, in an **accommodative approach**, managers make choices that try to balance the interests of shareholders with those of other stakeholders.

All of these approaches can be legal, but only one of them can protect your business when it comes to managing real risks, all the time. The obstructionist approach and the defensive approach are still gambling. We can't hedge our bets on cybersecurity.

What does this mean in real terms? It's about educating and aligning employees and contractors alike. What can you do?

- Educate employees on practices to improve risk management and seek out challenges before they become crises.

- Require contractors to implement practices consistent with company risk management policies and procedures, and allow them to speak up when challenges arise.

- Provide information and training for the safe handling of data and digital information of all kinds.

- Communicate openly and on a timely basis with employees, the public, governments, and other stakeholders on activities that have to do with risk management, privacy, and safety.

- Continue to strategically implement processes, practices, and technologies that will lead to improved cybersecurity and company safety performance.

- Conduct regular safety and emergency response audits, and implement action plans called for by these audits.

- Report regularly to the board of directors on risk management, safety, and emergency preparedness.

There are two great sources for supply chain risk management that can help you in this process. The first is from the New York State Department of Financial Services cybersecurity regulations, which contain a section on third-party vendor risk.[4] The other is from the U.K.'s National Cyber Security Centre principles of supply chain security.[5] Both are nontechnical guides to implementing what I call the three *p*'s of third-party risk: policies, prevention, and promises.

Policies: establish controls to manage vendor risk

- Define supply chain policies and revisit them on an annual basis.
- Develop due diligence tools to assess a vendor's security profile.
- Establish periodic validation to ensure the vendor's security program is working.
- Raise security awareness and share threat intelligence across your supply chain.
- Encourage improvement and open dialogue.

Prevention: measure and mitigate vendor risk

- Identify assets and obligations and consider the movement of confidential and protected information across your supply chain.
- Define your risk appetite to determine what services you are willing to outsource.
- Conduct risk assessments to measure your risk profile.
- Analyze results and risks and adjust your plans accordingly.
- Define defensive requirements that cover all tiers of your supply chain.

Promises: employee and contractor obligations

- Make contractual obligations to govern supply chain conduct.
- Demarcate responsibilities so all parties know their roles and responsibilities.
- Establish minimum standards for all elements of the supply chain.
- Set document notification requirements, reportable elements, triggers, and timelines.
- Give representations and warranties to provide indemnification and required insurance coverage.

At the end of the day with the Deepwater Horizon spill, multiple investigations faulted the well owner, BP; the drilling operator, Transocean; and a contractor, Halliburton. BP ultimately pleaded guilty to eleven counts of manslaughter and a felony count for lying to the U.S. Congress. In 2012, BP agreed to $4.5 billion in fines to settle with the Department of Justice. A further $18.7 billion was paid to settle a 2015 U.S. District Court decision that BP's gross negligence and reckless conduct were the primary culprits in the oil spill. Estimates from 2018 put the total costs to the company around $65 billion. As part of the settlement, BP published the findings of their investigation. The official report contains the findings of a four-month investigation conducted by more than fifty internal and external engineering specialists and experts.

There is no turning a blind eye. Mitigating risk in business requires setting aside a gambling mentality entirely. Whether transparency takes place inside or outside the company, we have to start looking at the world from the perspective of all stakeholders so that we are better able to achieve our goals. The implication is that to do right by our companies, we have to do right by every person who interacts with us.

Keeping on highest possible ethical road is the only way to stay safe from the highwaymen who take the low road.

8

GRAY CRIME
AND PUNISHMENT

MATTHEW FALDER CREATED a safe place in which to share sadistic "hurtcore" material on the dark web.

Falder wasn't what you would expect on the surface. He was a Cambridge scholar, brilliant in his own right, but he was a man who shared images of people in a way designed to cause them pain and anguish. Falder was said to have had more than fifty victims, but we know that he had approached more than two hundred people over the course of his criminal career. He specifically hunted out individuals and lured them into sending him photographs and videos by promising cash in return, and then blackmailed these parties when they did what he asked. He encouraged people to do both illegal and humiliating acts in the process, especially preying on young women. Falder then posted these images on dark web forums for pedophiles and sadists, and he provided advice to these people on how to avoid getting caught for engaging in the activities that he had psychologically abused and coerced them into doing in the first place.

The primary crimes that Falder committed were possession of pedophilia material, child sexual abuse, and blackmail going back to at least 2009. He committed crimes, targeted at both personal and corporate victims, by posing as a female artist on the internet, and by using thirty different encrypted email addresses so that he could not be easily traced. He posted on the dark web under three different usernames, which made it difficult to find him. He also had cameras installed at eight different locations, which allowed him to engage with thirteen victims in real life (as opposed to on the web). The psychological and financial consequences for victims of Falder's crimes were significant. Some victims attempted suicide multiple times and others were dealing with feeling "dirty, like used goods." Others have described feeling physically ill and unable to work as a result of Falder's manipulation.[1]

Falder was wanted for crimes in both the United States and the United Kingdom, but even under the observation of a global taskforce specifically devised to bring him down, he could not be found for almost a decade.

Why aren't we stopping these attacks?

If you commit a murder or rape, engage in human trafficking, or hold up a store with a gun, you're going to go directly to jail. Particularly heinous crimes warrant severe penalties on par across most countries. The chair of the American Bar Association, in a conversation a couple of years ago, referred to this as the international leveling of punishment.

In some cases, governments would rather not prosecute, such as in the case of cyber-espionage and nation-state (or state-sponsored) attacks. Why? Because both sides are participating in similar behavior, just for their own means, and they need, superficially, to pretend that it isn't happening in order to protect their own assets in the field. To some degree, we are living in a cyber-version of the cold war, with its protagonist West (the United States, United Kingdom, and other European allies) and antagonist East (Communist Bloc countries led by the Soviet Union). Back then, the Americans had their spies in Moscow, and the Russians had their reciprocal secret representatives in Washington, D.C. Each country knew who the spies were, CIA and KGB alike. But each side observed an unwritten détente, understanding that actions warranted equal and opposite reactions. For example, if one side grabbed a known spy and went to work on them with a rubber hose or other form of torture, then the other side would grab a spy in their capital and do the same to them. So both sides observed a code of conduct and looked for advantage in less kinetic ways than arresting spies and risking a not-so-cold war.

But let's set aside espionage for a moment.

In our cyber world, there are few rules and fewer convictions, and neither national nor international laws can keep up. Individuals involved in these crimes may be living outside the jurisdiction of prosecutors, which means it may be difficult to ensure that they can be brought to justice without cooperation from international agencies and other nations. The cooperation of international law enforcement, and INTERPOL warrants especially, can take months to deploy, giving the criminals ample getaway time. The anonymous nature of the crime combined with the lack of access to criminals can make this a difficult situation for all involved.

This is why organized crime is invested in cybercrime. Using a computer to steal money is much easier than robbing a bank. To rob a bank, you can use a cool code name, don an ironic mask, and likely get shot in the process of the robbery. Or at least go to jail.[2] With cyber fraud, you can buy readily accessible tools to rob faceless people on the other side of the world, and you can still use a cool code name and don an ironic mask if you want. According to the FBI's *2010 Internet Crime Report*, nearly 304,000 cyber fraud complaints led to just 1,400 criminal cases (far less than 1 percent) and six convictions—one for every 51,000 victims. Robbing a bank nets you a one in four chance of doing hard time.[3]

In the United States, the Department of Justice's *Criminal Resource Manual* defines computer crime as "any illegal act for which knowledge of computer technology is essential for successful prosecution."[4] Nonetheless, some of the problems in pursuing an effective prosecution involve the fact that cybernetworks are so deeply difficult to infiltrate, and many of them are even automated, which means that it becomes difficult to trace the crime back to a single location or person. They also overlap. Cybercrime can involve identity theft, embezzlement, fraud, and outright theft. This can take place via malicious code, a distributed denial-of-service attack, spam fraud, or phishing for information from vulnerable people such as older adults. In some cases, door-to-door culprits wearing Home Depot painting coveralls and protective face gear masqueraded as Red Cross workers offering COVID-19 home-testing kits.[5] It can also involve higher level financial fraud such as corporate security breaches, piracy, and large-scale consumer information theft that can put millions of people at risk at the same time. Cybercrime can be committed through the use of fraud, deception, or collusion, and it can include activities such as money laundering or organizational fraud, committed on the behalf of a client as well as for personal gain.

Or it can be a solitary attack on a single, vulnerable human being.

Lawmakers are beginning to propose and pass more cybercrime security legislation, but a lot of it feels like too little, too late.

Part of this has to do with the ways in which cybercrime and white-collar crime are often linked. The same patterns of virtual crime can be found in large-scale legitimate businesses as in black market operations, and some of these crimes are also connected to funding terrorism. As terrorists develop a more diffuse, insulated network structure, for example, the individual cells are increasingly left to their own devices to raise funds. Many of these organizations have legally established front businesses, and can use these businesses to commit white-collar cybercrime to collect money to fund their ideological aims. As well, at both ends of the organizational spectrum—from the largest and most overt global businesses to those that are the most hidden—globalization is changing the way that business is being conducted and being made secret. Multinational companies often employ a so-called race-to-the-bottom approach so that they can drive down the costs of doing business and use tax havens to hide their assets. Think Mossack Fonseca at the heart of the Panama Papers scandal. As a result, any new regulations created to curb these activities may not be easily applied, especially internationally.

What's a real crime, anyway?

All of this is complicated by the fact that, until very recently, much of what we know as cybercrime was not perceived to be "real" crime. The general public doesn't always perceive that many of these crimes are, indeed, criminal.

Let's take piracy as an example. Recently, the Business Software Alliance reported that 37 percent of software (worth $43.6 billion) is illegally copied per year.[6] They reported on the hypothetical value of lost sales of their intellectual property, not on the loss of the worth of the plastic discs they used to ship to computer stores. The concept of wealth itself is increasingly represented in nonphysical units, and people often don't think twice about downloading pirated software, movies, or music. Even though the ongoing challenge for criminals is that the media has ensured that it is more difficult for these kinds of crimes to be perpetuated, the issue of cybercrime is bigger than we understand. The complexity of crime and its effects on people's choices in the present day, therefore, influence what we pressure our governments to do—and to make illegal.

Of course, corporations are going to lobby for changes to the law, but even there the line is blurred. Those who work within organizations and commit fraud on their own behalf or that of their clients, as well as those who employ white-collar crime techniques on their own, do not necessarily believe that they are committing true crimes. The Association of Certified Fraud Examiners, for example, notes that in the United States and Canada, corporate billing schemes outnumber cybersecurity schemes by a significant amount. Out of the cases that they have examined, billing frauds *authorized by companies* were reported in 20 percent of the U.S. cases, which is significantly higher than the level of corruption that was perpetrated by individuals trying to get one over on their employer.[7] The underlying challenge is, of course, our acceptance of social values that permit businesses a great deal of ethical leeway to make profits.

In other words, we're all complicit. We're all a part of this massive push to allow the boundaries of what's considered right and wrong to slide, and we've gotten caught up in it. We're not certain, at any given point, where we need to be to ensure we're safe and secure.

But cybercrime also pays for good hiding places.

Let's take Silk Road, the now-defunct illegal drug website, which was run by a man named Ross Ulbricht, who used the online moniker The Dread Pirate Roberts. He counted on the use of a bidding-style escrow system and Bitcoin bank, in which users had to give up controls of their Silk Road banking accounts until a transaction had cleared. It took two years for the FBI to finally shut down the online drug marketplace and prosecute Ulbricht. But he stayed hidden until 2013 for the simple reason that he had a lot of money, and demand for his products was so high that no one was willing to reveal his whereabouts. The way in which these crimes are identified and prosecuted is essentially the same as the way in which in-person frauds are pursued, but the reality is that the individuals who run these schemes can and will be located anywhere in cyberspace, and therefore anywhere in the world.

So, now our laws are getting tighter

Singapore is a leader in bringing world leaders together to try to get the ball rolling on enforceable international legislation and coordinated discovery and prosecution of cybercriminals. As a hyperconnected global business and financial hub, Singapore has been a huge target for hackers. To that end, they've signed a memorandum of understanding with the United States, South Korea, New Zealand, Canada, India, Australia, France, the Netherlands, and the United Kingdom to ensure that we're all working from the same handbook on cybersecurity. Even though those perpetrating these crimes may be living outside the jurisdiction of the prosecutors in the country pursuing them, the level of cooperation from these nations to directly go after cybercrime networks has increased.

Closer to home, changes are also taking place, and rapidly. Senator Jerry Moran (R-Kansas), chairman of the Commerce Subcommittee on Consumer Protection, introduced the

Consumer Data Privacy and Security Act of 2020. In 2019, the U.S. Congress introduced the Internet of Things Cybersecurity Improvement Act. In 2018, California became the first state to pass IoT cybersecurity laws. Industry regulators such as the SEC have worked with the Securities Industry and Financial Markets Association (SIFMA) to now require brokers, dealers, mutual funds sellers, and other financial institutions to more deeply "understand the nature and purpose of customer relationships for the purpose of developing a customer risk profile and conduct ongoing monitoring to identify and report suspicious transactions."[8] They're doing this to require financial institutions to become their first-line watchdogs to see if anything is raising suspicions on the ground floor. The New York State Department of Financial Services is also requiring all banks and money managers to become alert to nation-states, terrorist organizations, and independent criminal actors and the threat that they pose to their clients, and to the state.

And let's talk about privacy laws as well. Europe and California are in the lead in this regard with General Data Protection Regulation and the California Consumer Privacy Act, respectively. Other states, including Hawaii, Maryland, Massachusetts, New York, and North Dakota, are eyeing legislation similar to California's, which came into effect in 2020. For privacy to be protected for consumers, to shield them from both corporate misuse of data and the potential threat of hackers, several elements must be included in these policies. These include technological application laws and guidelines, policies for how people share data, processes that are permitted and not permitted by corporations, as well as guidelines and recommended business strategies. It comes down to three core ideas:

1   People have the right to privacy protection either by not being active participants online or by limiting the ways in which they choose to interact with websites, such as by

refusing to accept cookies or shutting down push notification options, or the right to be forgotten, if they withdraw their online participation.

2   Internet service providers have to provide the backbone for privacy by creating firewalls between data sources.

3   Online software creators, including the companies who create websites, who develop and sell the means to package data, have to create internal barriers in their code.

GDPR also requires private data to be processed with transparency, inaccurate data to be deleted or changed within a swift time period, and all companies to be accountable and able to demonstrate compliance with the other personal data processing principles. This means that corporations are likely to have to decide on their own how and when to use data that could compromise the ethical standard for privacy. This is the case, even though this data could be used to monitor, sell to, control, and steal from individuals, especially because of the dearth of federal legal or regulatory controls in place in the United States to protect the privacy of individuals in an online environment.

To help us meet the laws and regulations that are already in place, cybersecurity experts have created specification standards that we can count on as a first step down the road to risk management. Security policy has to be focused on trust, information protection, and access control rules. These standards define requirements that enforce security policies developed by IT departments. For example, ISO/IEC 27001 is a best-practice information security management system that can measure, review, assess, and adjust organizational confidentiality, integrity, and availability standards. As well, the National Institute of Standards and Technology has created a cybersecurity framework, which can be used voluntarily, to decrease cybersecurity risk for critical infrastructure.

The mighty fail

The challenge with U.S. federal law as it stands is that it can lead to what is known as the personalization privacy paradox.

Current cybersecurity policies presented by the largest organizations, such as Apple and Google, which are responsible for much of the searching that people engage in on the internet, suggest that the privacy of their customers is assured, including even privacy protection from the U.S. government. But this is not the case. Google, for example, accounts for 70 percent of the search market in the United States, and it keeps historical data on its users' searches, which it then uses in several different ways, including predicting user search intentions, expected results, and macro search trends. Here's how these companies get around the challenge of rectifying their actions: their terms and conditions are tied to what is known as personalization. When an individual takes part in an Apple or Google system experience, for example, such as the use of iTunes or Gmail, their receiving of a free or low-cost service is tied to the ability of the organization to use push notifications that, superficially, provide users with information on services or products that are linked to their needs. Nonetheless, personalization often goes far beyond a consumer's needs, offering them the same products over and over again, even after they have been purchased. And the companies are allowed to take, use, and store consumer buying and search preferences because there are no legal barriers or regulations in place.

What does that mean for the average company? Many business leaders aim to emulate Apple and Google. I get it. They make good money. But the thing is, when we play these kinds of games, we learn quickly that there is a disconnect between the idea that eased privacy permissions leads to better usability for consumers and the idea that an individual's privacy can be protected. That's the paradox. Do you have the money, legal standing, and temerity to even start going down that road?

We measure human progress in terms of anthropological or historical ages. Stone Age, Bronze Age, Middle Ages, and so on. We measure technical progress in terms of industrial revolutions: mechanization with steam and water, mass production, and more. So, what will we call this age in which you are the product *and* the consumer?

The consumer *is* the product. That's not a drug-fueled quote from the likes of Hunter S. Thompson or Lewis Carroll. It's the house of mirrors in which we live now. We give away our identity with a click of "I agree," and then buy it back in the form of products aligned to our searches, preferences, and social media brags. Marshall McLuhan, you were right: The medium is the message. Now the medium and message are us. There is no line by which we delineate.

And let's not forget that cyber service providers are pushing more responsibility for security onto users. By that, I don't mean your customers alone. I mean your business: the entity using third-party software, online stores, and web tools of all kinds. What happens, as well, when the "user" is a device itself, like an RFID device? All we know is that security tensions can multiply and increase the complexity of an already complex user environment, leading to massive security risks.

It's your responsibility to keep up using the National Association of Corporate Directors's five pillars of risk management, which I introduced in chapter 2. The onus is on businesses—on you—to ensure your own and your clients' data is safe. Hacked businesses and their leaders need to protect themselves not only from litigation but from breaking all of these newly emerging laws and regulations.

The law *is* catching up, not just to careless businesses but to criminals as well. And people are being caught and prosecuted.

Just as it took a long time to find him, it will likely take a great deal of time for the full impact of Matthew Falder's crimes on his victims to be addressed, but in 2018 he was charged with 188 counts for crimes taking place between 2009 and 2017, and he pled guilty to 137 of these against forty-six victims.[9] It is likely that, given that he has admitted to most of the crimes already, Falder will spend the rest of his life in prison. It is important to note, as well, that in pursuing justice against Falder, the prosecution has also been able to rout a number of his conspirators on the dark web, and there will likely be numerous subsequent arrests.

Let's hope so.

9

NO ONE HAS YOUR BACK

BUYING BITCOIN ISN'T quite the same as exchanging dollars for euros.

Bitcoin is a currency that is not issued by an official financial authority. It's a system rather than a true currency, offering peer-to-peer online payments without using a traditional financial institution as an intermediary. This new system of digital payments uses a shared protocol based on encryption techniques, which means that there are locks and steps to get your money and to use it. A public blockchain is considered to be a large, unforgeable ledger, freely accessible to a network's users all over the world. In 2008, Satoshi Nakamoto linked such a chain to the digital currency he called Bitcoin. But most financial leaders refer to it as "inventive" money. As in not real, even though it is used more and more. In finance, for example, blockchain-based currencies like Bitcoin can be used to transfer assets like securities, shares, or bonds, rather than just money. Like paper money, its value is in what we believe it's worth. That's why Bitcoin is regularly used for transactions that operate outside the realm of legal activity.

But also, Bitcoin is complex because it's not so straightforward to obtain. First, you have to have a Bitcoin wallet set up. Then you have to get the Bitcoin into the wallet, but there are often delays. When you buy Bitcoin funds, the transaction needs to be recorded in the blockchain and affirmed, and sometimes there are limits on how many you can purchase in a day. Payments into and out of a Bitcoin account can be slow. It's possible to move fast, but you must have access, opportunity, and, of course, a lot of cash on hand.

So, in 2017, when a ten-person Rhode Island law firm, Moses Afonso Ryan, was sent a ransom for their files, and thirteen Bitcoins were demanded as payment, all of their client information ended up being shut down, completely inaccessible, for close to a year. A lot got in the way, and not just the ransom that they chose to pay. The law firm struggled with those financial transactions, but they also weren't getting what they needed from the hackers. The decryption tools they received when some of the money went through weren't effective. The cybersecurity experts they hired to fix the problem weren't able to access the files. And law enforcement could do little to find and prosecute the criminals responsible.

Moses Afonso Ryan paid $25,000 in ransom and lost an estimated $700,000 in billable hours (the metric by which law firms assess revenue), and so they made a claim for the latter with their insurer, Sentinel Risk Insurance Group. They had nowhere else to turn, and this attack had decimated their business equity and their potential for recovery. Although business income interruption was covered in the law firm's policy, Sentinel denied the claim.

The same stories have been repeated over and over again in recent years.

In 2019, the Vancouver, Canada, branch of global law firm Dentons became locked in a court battle with their insurer,

Trisura Guarantee, when one of their legal associates was tricked into transferring $2.5 million into an unknown Hong Kong bank account, thinking that the money was going to pay off a client's mortgage. Having recovered $800,000 of the funds, Dentons was denied their insurance claim because Trisura suggested that Dentons had failed to add a social engineering fraud rider when they set up the policy. A ruling favored the insurer, and Dentons had to take the hit.

In 2017, furniture retailer The Brick was denied coverage from Chubb Insurance Company of Canada for the same reasons. Chubb hadn't set The Brick up with a policy to specifically cover phishing.

In 2017, as we've discussed, the Equifax breach led to the company's loss of data for 147 million consumers. They had $75 million in cybersecurity insurance paid up before the breach, but an expected $200 million in costs connected to the criminal event itself. Their claim for $275 million far exceeds what their insurers expect to pay.

Let's face facts. No insurance plan will truly cover you in the case of an attack. They will look for leaks within your company, your financial controls and security procedures, and whether you were aware or warned of risks and chose not to do everything you could to protect your company and your clients.

The world of cyber insurance is like the Wild West when it comes to determining risk and covering losses.

When insurance isn't ensured

In the past, insurance companies had long-term, predictable liabilities in mind when they decided what to charge and what they were going to pay for. Actuaries, the people who decide how much risk an insurance company can take on and, therefore, how much organizations should pay for that insurance, start the process with reams of data. Actuarial science is just that: a science, informed by futurist predictions and a lot of math, to try to ensure a balance that serves all parties is in place. Actuarial tables are legendary, and they've been around for centuries, drawing on human survival statistics, car accident rates, and the probability that your house will be set on fire by an arsonist.

The thing is, however, that the kind of probabilities that businesses face when it comes to cybersecurity are almost impossible to determine. Try to run the math on whether one specific organization will have their business interrupted, lose revenue, and pay out for extortion costs. How much will they lose directly? Through payouts to their affected clients or fighting class action lawsuits? How long will their business leak information, have to shut down, and pay out severance packages to a bulk number of employees? What will their incident response expenses be, including emergency cybersecurity support? Will they pay any fines for breaking regulations?

This list gets bigger and bigger the more complex cybersecurity becomes, and the more our governments and justice agencies become limited in what they can do to address the issue through legal processes. This is not even taking into account the massive challenges that organizations could face if a cybersecurity attack, such as the ones we've discussed in this book, is linked to terrorism or nation-state attacks.

Some companies, such as AIG, are trying to work directly with their clients to continuously monitor their risk. This is a means to hold clients to their word, and their work, of getting set up to stop an attack before it happens. But even with this much one-on-one support, premiums are going up, and even with the best of intentions and cybersecurity operations, this upward trajectory for insurance costs isn't likely to change.[1]

With 23 percent of Americans already affected by cybercrime in some way, there's no way for insurance companies to continue to have control over their predictions. All of a sudden, they, like us, don't know what's going to happen next.

As a result, the American Academy of Actuaries are telling it like it is. They have stated that insurance company expenses for cybersecurity will likely continue to outpace revenues in the system, and therefore that the whole insurance system may break down. As they write, "Within auto or property insurance companies, substantial data exists on accidents, and actuaries can calculate the risks, prices, and reserves necessary. However, there is far less data on cyber risks because data breaches are relatively new, which makes calculating prices and reserves more difficult. Insurance prices set too high will limit the number of businesses that find coverage economical or individuals who can afford coverage, while prices that are too low could lead to insurers not being able to pay all claims."[2] In other words, there may be nothing that insurance companies can do to either predict these crimes or defend their clients from their effects, without being taken down in the fray.

Consider the alternative investment market, for example. It's made up of thousands of smaller funds, commonly known as hedge funds, that control large amounts of money more akin to something a large bank would manage. Hedge funds measure their size in terms of the money they manage, referred to as assets under management. These firms, with anywhere between twenty-five and five hundred employees, manage investments ranging in value from $250 million to billions of dollars. The money they manage comes from institutional investors like pension funds and wealthy individuals who invest sums on the scale of an average of $150 million each.

These organizations can be toppled by their investors. If, for example, the fund were to experience a significant cyberattack and lose tens of millions of dollars, this could unsettle the investors, who would demand their money back in a request for redemption. Like runs on banks in the Great Depression, large numbers of requests for redemption can cause these funds to go insolvent and disappear overnight. How does an insurance company build algorithms that can predict these types of lightning strikes? And what do you insure? The $10 million that was lost to cyber criminals? Or the value of the defunct hedge fund, in the order of $500 million? It's clearly not economically plausible to insure such an enormous sum, as the premiums would likely rival the amount of money under the fund's management. In the end, these funds simply acquire policies to cover investigation costs and client notification. It all feels a little anemic in the face of a corporate-extinction-level event.

You can't insure your reputation

Beyond cost, consider another dimension: reputation. Think about LeMessurier in the Citicorp story earlier in this book. He knew his reputation was at risk once he exposed the design flaw in his brand-new Manhattan tower. Likewise on a spring flight to the Midwest, the crew of an airliner learned that a reputation is difficult to build, but all too easy to destroy.

On April 4, 1979, Trans World Airlines (TWA) Flight 841 was en route from New York JFK to Minneapolis. Somewhere over Michigan, the Boeing 727 aircraft began to bank wildly to the right. Captain Harvey "Hoot" Gibson and his experienced crew fought to regain control of the plane as it made two complete 360-degree barrel rolls and lost 34,000 feet of altitude in just over one minute, which must have resulted in a lifetime of terror for the passengers. At five thousand feet, the pilots finally wrested control of the 727 and made an emergency landing at the Detroit Metropolitan Airport forty-five minutes later. There were no fatalities, and only eight passengers suffered minor injuries during the incident. The subsequent investigation determined that the result of the accident was due to pilot error, and worse, a cover-up on the part of the flight crew.

The National Transportation Safety Board (NTSB) found that the incident occurred because of a wing slat being out of place, and the board leaned heavily on the aircraft manufacturer's determination that it could only have been out of place because the crew intentionally set it that way. A recognized rumor at the time was that to increase flight speed without increasing fuel usage pilots would slightly raise these slats, though they were not designed for mid-flight use. The NTSB also latched onto a missing portion of the cockpit voice recorder (CVR) tape, presumed deleted by the flight crew to hide their dangerous actions. The press jumped on this supposed conspiracy and the crew were found guilty in the court of public opinion, regardless of the fact that the missing portion of the recording had nothing to do with the emergency portion of the flight, and the CVR can only be erased when the plane is on the ground and the parking brake is engaged. There was no way to erase the tape mid-flight.

In a later interview with CBS, Captain Gibson quipped that having Boeing conduct the airframe investigation was akin to "putting Dracula in charge of the blood bank."[3] The aircraft was repaired and went back into service, but Captain Gibson's reputation was destroyed forever, and the ghost of this event and the findings of NTSB haunted his career to the end. For over a decade, he fought to clear his name.[4] He appealed the NTSB's findings within their mechanism, and later to the U.S. Court of Appeals for the Ninth Circuit. Both petitions were rejected. Gibson felt peers never believed his version of events and assumed he and his flight crew were "screwing around with the controls." While Gibson continued to fly for TWA for period of time, he claimed that multiple flight attendants refused to fly with him, and on one occasion this mistrust forced him to return to the gate with a planeload of passengers to disembark a fearful flight attendant.[5]

No one has your back. And insurance can't protect, repair, or replace your reputation. As Benjamin Franklin observed, "It takes many good deeds to build a reputation, and only one bad one to lose it."[6] You simply can't insure whether people trust you. At the heart of the Panama Papers scandal, Mossack Fonseca closed its doors entirely after being exposed to cybercrime, blaming the "reputational deterioration" and other factors that occasioned "irreversible damage that necessitates the obligatory ceasing of public operations."[7]

The value and the gotchas of cyber policies

A few short years ago, organizations in all industries took a hands-up approach. They focused on building disaster recovery programs, invested in backup systems to restore post attack, and bought cyber insurance, assuming it would cover the damage. And they were wrong. It was like driving down the road with your eyes closed because, after all, you have auto insurance that will cover medical and vehicular damage. Who in their right mind would do this? Great, the two years of medical rehab is financially covered. But what about the pain? What about irreversible damage and resulting disability? What about the safety of other motorists? It's an insane prospect.

But that's exactly what businesses did. Closed their eyes, prayed for the best, and had their insurance brokers on speed dial.

Cyber insurance is intended to cover the immediate losses resulting from cyber incidents that aren't necessarily covered by other products such as business disruption. Liabilities are generally categorized as first party (that's you, the policy holder) and third party (that's anyone affected, like clients or employees). In general, cyber insurance will cover specific losses, investigation, and cleanup costs, and notification to clients and affected parties. It won't cover penalties levied by regulators or state-level privacy laws. Just like your auto insurance, cyber insurance won't cover your speeding tickets.[8]

Here's what we're talking about in most policies.

First-party liability

- Business interruption costs, including lost revenue during a forced outage
- Repairs to IT infrastructure and reconstituting data
- Breach notification expenses incurred communicating to clients, regulators, and your supply chain
- Forensic investigation costs determining the root cause, scope, and remediation efforts required by the event (this is often provided by a specialized organization)

Legal expenses

- Public relations and crisis management efforts (again, often provided by a specialized PR organization)
- Regulatory defense expenses associated with the investigation of a regulatory event—but not the fine itself

Third-party liability

- Credit monitoring costs required to detect credit fraud or provide credit scores for a fixed period of time (twelve to twenty-four months)
- Privacy or claims brought against the organization by employees, clients, or business partners
- Business interruption claims filed by affected third parties
- Media liability damages resulting from claims for libel, slander, defamation, copyright infringement, and so on

Force majeure definitions have yet to be tested, but will likely have their day in court, post COVID-19 outbreak. Cyber insurance policies rarely cover regulatory fines or acts of war and terrorism, just like more common forms of insurance. And closer to home, these policies don't necessarily cover monetary or trading losses, and definitely don't cover losses resulting from reputational damage.

When organizations are denied coverage under their cyber insurance policy, it's like adding insult to injury. It's tough to be the victim of a cyberattack, punished by a regulator for good measure, and then, on top of everything else, your insurance won't cover your real-cost expenses and losses.[9]

Some of the most common claim denials come from a small set of causes.

Failure to maintain refers to negligence or "failure to follow" exclusions within the policy that bind the insured party to maintain minimum or adequate security standards. It's like if you don't put oil in your car's engine on the manufacturer's specified schedule: when the engine ceases to work, your auto insurance won't cover it because of your perceived neglect. This failure can also extend to noncompliant operations that violate regulatory rules in financial or health care businesses. So, if you fail to meet HIPAA standards, you might lose your insurance coverage.

Regulatory fines or assessments are often denied as part of the coverage. For example, the U.S. restaurant chain PF Chang's received $2 million to cover the costs resulting from the exposure of millions of customers' credit card information. But a further $2 million was denied, as it related to Payment Card Industry Data Security Standard fines and assessments (mandated operational improvements).

Cyber extortion and ransomware are as commonplace as we've discussed, but not always covered in a blanket cyber insurance policy. There is the ransom itself (assuming it's paid), but also resulting operational disruption, cleanup, and lost revenue. Remember the small law firm in Rhode Island? They lost $700,000 in billable hours, but only recovered $20,000 to cover system damage. Always address ransomware with your broker to clearly delineate what expenses and losses are covered.

Social engineering schemes are as commonplace as ransomware, yet often do not yield insurance payouts. The most common scheme is the kind of business email compromise we've previously discussed, where fraudulent invoices are paid out. In many cases, including Dentons, coverage is denied because the unwitting employees circumvented security protocols, and the money was "voluntarily" paid by an authorized employee with access to the protected systems required to make electronic fund transfers. While this is technically a "failure to maintain," insurance companies call out specific tactics, such as ransomware and email fraud, as nonrecoverable through insurance payout. Or, they require a specific rider in the policy that covers payouts for these eventualities.

We cannot predict what we cannot imagine

Often there are unintended consequences to our actions. Take, for example, the story of the fitness tracking app Strava. Smart and connected devices allow us to tap metrics critical to improving our health and maximizing the output of our workouts. And, of course, in an interconnected world, we share this data. It's an omni-peer presentation of our performance. Strava created maps that showed the compiled efforts and tracked running routes of its users, including a large contingent of military personnel. And in doing so, it unintentionally created inferential maps of secret U.S. military bases.[10] A simple exercise app had undone all the work of the military to protect its personnel from enemy interference.

You can keep track of risks, review your exposure, and address gaps that you can see, but the reality of the present-day hacking environment is that no one has your back, except you and your own organizational team. And you have to be prepared to address the unseen or unpredicted.

Leadership is crucial, because without any substantive backup, you're the only guardians of your threshold. It's up to you, and no one else.

Companies often don't see things this way, because we're all used to a simpler way of doing things. Some people within the organization may raise the alarm about your IT or security behavior practices that could have a negative long-term effect. The challenge is that leaders may ignore this information because they want to believe that the company will be fine without spending money on any substantive changes to the status quo. Information may be very clearly pointing towards a different set of actions, but these facts may be set aside because they are seen as something that happens to other companies and other people. Organizations, and their leaders, can become used to being able to make money and the idea that they are too big or too small to lose and, therefore, lose sight of what has changed in the world around them. They sometimes think big teeth trumps short forearms, and miss the fact that the tyrannosaurus rex was outlived by its tiny mammal competitors.

This kind of attitude makes an organization desperate. And it ensures that an organization lacks the creativity, and the capacity, to look at what may be coming.

And, critically, we don't know what's coming. Lawmakers don't know; insurers don't know.

You're going to have to think about displacing your cybersecurity risks as gearing up for a battle. There are no pieces of information, or people, that you can afford to ignore. Everyone has to be in this together. How will you ensure your team is ready for a breach? Experimentation with specification-based intrusion detection is needed to prove that a proposed security framework is working correctly. As security policies are tested, collected data can be analyzed to verify what's working and what's not. This use of data may be able to prove the value of the security framework by observing when a set of resources changes to different security values. For example, running incident simulations to test readiness, and reviewing publicly available threat intelligence helps quantify stolen data value. Doing so means that organizations can determine where resources, policies, and procedures need to be placed to best secure present and future systems. This is not only to protect the customers of the company but also to ensure that evidence of the crime is preserved, if there is a breach.

And if there is a breach? The observe-orient-decide-act (OODA) approach is used by most American military combat operations to defeat an adversary and survive. It depends on ongoing observation and analysis of a situation, and a process that has been adopted and mastered by all team members. It requires an information system that can supply up-to-the-minute information about the business, its competitors, and the environment in which it operates.

What's first in your OODA loop?

1 **OBSERVE.** What's happening right now that you need to address? What's your identification- and evidence-recovery process?

2 **ORIENT.** A multilevel response and command structure has to be called up and briefed on what you've observed. Who are your key leaders, right now, and are they in the office? The roles needed for a coordinated response process include those responsible for tactical management of the

cybercrime and investigation management of the threat. Where are they? What resources are available to you right now? Do you have your response plan set up, and are you orienting all team members to what is happening next?

3 **DECIDE.** Once everyone is briefed, this is when critical decisions are made. What has to happen first? Who needs to know? When must you call in the police or other authorities?

4 **ACT.** Here's where you provide media and public information management for clients. But you also need to ensure that there is management of support services for all units involved in the breach. All of these individual units must report to a strategic command center in which operations are evaluated and led.

Measurements can help obtain a more complete and thorough understanding of the system and framework, but client communication will also be a key factor in ongoing success after a breach has occurred. What are you going to say to your clients? How can you show that you were prepared and were not at fault? How can you protect yourself financially and reputationally?

If you wait until after a breach has taken place, you'll also be past the point of making internal fixes, and you will have to make bold moves to save your organization from its eventual destruction. In fact, you may have to take more risks in order to avoid the impact of the risks you didn't address earlier. Think about the fallout: layoffs or divestments, liquidation of assets, or even organizational destruction.

If you can't plan ahead, the worst will happen. If you think insurance will provide some form of soft landing, think again.

10

THE NEXT WAR

N 2017, CHARLOTTESVILLE, Virginia, was home to one of the largest rallies for white supremacy that had taken place in the United States in history. Bringing together the alt right, neo-Nazis, and the Ku Klux Klan, the protest against the replacing of the statue of Confederate general Robert E. Lee ended up creating a state of emergency under the command of the governor of the state. Even though there were merely a few hundred protesters in place, individuals carrying "torches, homemade shields, weapons and Confederate and Nazi flags" ended up with a car plowing "into a crowd of peaceful counter-protesters, killing one person and injuring nineteen."[1] The rise of white supremacist, neo-Nazi, anti-Semitic, and racist rhetoric in public marks a sea change in the direction of social values in the United States over the last fifty years, wherein a new form of nationalism has emerged, and which suggests that there are direct challenges to peaceful dialogue on social, cultural, and political differences that have begun to take over the internet.[2]

These are not faraway terrorists. But they are completely embedded in a multinational, underground world that is employing cybercrime to extort money, and gain support and power along the way, so that they can change our world to one that they have imagined is possible.

Andrew Anglin's Daily Stormer website was created in 2014 based on Nazi Julius Streicher's anti-Semitic weekly newspaper, *Der Stürmer*, a tabloid that was prevalent in the 1930s and 1940s that specialized in presenting pornographic attacks on Jewish people to deliberately defame them. Anglin worked with Andrew Auernheimer, aka "Weev," a neo-Nazi hacker and troll. Auernheimer was webmaster for the Daily Stormer after he was let out of federal prison in 2014, having served a sentence for identity theft and hacking. Both were Americans, but Anglin was living in an undisclosed area of Europe and Auernheimer in Transnistria, a region of Moldova that received Russian funding.[3] Interestingly enough, however, Anglin was not always a white supremacist, and reports about his youth are marked by both an outspoken liberal and vegan ideology and a penchant for public self-harm.[4]

It wasn't just the website that they were creating, however. It was a movement. The 2017 rally was known conventionally as the Unite the Right rally, but it had little to do with conventional politics. The two Andrews sought out involvement from groups such as Vanguard America, Traditionalist Worker Party, National Socialist Movement, League of the South, and former Klansman David Duke, as well as Richard Spencer and Mike "Enoch" Peinovich from the alt-right blogosphere.[5] The purpose in planning the rally was to unite the various social splinters of right-wing Americans against those that they hated. It likely didn't go as planned. The Daily Stormer was removed from active online space as a result of Anglin's participation in the rally, and because of the fact that it celebrated the death of the protester Heather Heyer at that event.[6] Anglin's online property has been banned by its internet service provider, and by Facebook, Google Domains, and YouTube, and as a result only operates on the dark web.

But that's where things continued to get worse. With their move underground, the two Andrews were able to plead for support from those who backed their cause without being tracked. Auernheimer and Anglin started soliciting cyber-stalking support from all over the world, targeting University of Missouri students; American University's first black woman student-body president; and Erin Schrode, a Jewish woman running for Congress, while simultaneously teaching all of their followers to cover their digital tracks. They received money from fans and other trolls, from the KKK, and by some accounts, from the Russian Federation government.

The two Andrews, as well as others aligned with their cause, lurk in the background of society, congratulating each other on their ability to understand the "real" truth of white supremacy and their perceived need to destroy others. It is not entirely clear, given what we know about Andrew Anglin in particular, whether he is in fact the ultimate troll or an extremist who is bent on eradicating whole peoples and religions from Earth.

The only thing that the law has been able to do to address these despicable acts is to allow a civil case against Anglin to go forward. Despite the fact that, in 2019, he was ordered to pay $14 million for urging followers to terrorize Tanya Gersh, a Jewish woman in Montana, Anglin is still at the forefront of the white supremacy movement. And his whereabouts are unknown. He has never appeared in court, even though there was a flock of lawyers there, paid by his supporters, to try to clear him.

No matter how deep on the web his site is located, it does not bode well.

There is no collateral damage, there's just damage

The reality that we now face is that threat landscape is constantly changing, and the invisible world of cyberspace is filled with people who have one goal: to exploit others.

Cybercriminals may hack a company for the purpose of taking it offline for a single day so that they can short their stock and come up large in the markets. They may want to shift trading around the world in a single industry, or change the outcomes of an election, to further the interests of a nation-state. They may want to kick off a global health care crisis by changing the ingredients in a drug that keeps millions of people alive every day.

We simply don't know what the next attack will be. Think about what could happen if any cybergroup became organized. As people turn more and more to social media sources for news and for information on topical issues, the line between what we know and what we think is true begins to blur. What happens with smaller hate groups, in real, practical terms, is not much different than the kind of nation-state attacks we talked about earlier in this book, because there is no longer a line between combatants and civilian actors. Cybercrime is all about destruction and the forced reordering of what we know and expect about our daily lives.

Let's look at what the Council on Foreign Relations has to say. They expect that the level of nation-state cyberattacks is going to increase. We are potentially already seeing the signs: Bolivia's recent election was plagued by accusations of election fraud and China has been accused of turning their "Great Cannon" against the LIHKG forum used by Hong Kong protesters to coordinate their protests against the Beijing government. In fact, the U.S. government has indicted members of China's military on charges of hacking Equifax and "plundering sensitive data on nearly 150 million Americans as part of a massive heist that also stole trade secrets from the credit reporting agency."[7]

We operate in a constantly connected and virtual world, where politics, economics, and business are intertwined like weather, the seasons, and the climate. Remember chaos theory and the hurricane-generating butterfly? That notion applies here too. But in reverse. Tectonic political motions can create microquakes across the globe that often fail to register on the Richter scale of mass media, yet have significant consequences for those directly affected.

Events such as the airstrikes by the United States that killed Iranian General Qasem Soleimani on January 3, 2020, and the responding January 8 Iran-launched missiles that struck an Iraqi base where U.S. personnel were stationed, are such a case. These macro events often herald the beginning of increased efforts by known threat actors and groups with ties to Iran that choose cyber targets of opportunity for economic gain or to cause chaos under the banner of righteous revenge. It's less about their political agenda, like those that defaced multiple U.S. government sites, but rather about how hacks against banks, law firms, and hospitals negatively impact the business and harm their clients and patients.

Gray crime for profit

In season two of the Showtime hit *Billions*, we find the feud between Bobby "Axe" Axelrod, the founder of the huge hedge fund Axe Capital, and the district attorney Chuck Rhoades comes to a crescendo when Axelrod plots to tank an upcoming public offering of stock in a new juice company. Axelrod knows that Rhoades, his allies, and family are overextended on the deal. Axelrod hires actors to fake violent illnesses when they consume their Ice Juice drinks on the day of the initial public offering. News of a nasty bacteria in drinks travels fast through social channels, and the stock that launched at $20 a share quickly starts plummeting. Trading is halted and frozen at a meager $3 a share. It's "Armageddon" as Rhoades realizes his multimillion-dollar loss.

It's fiction, but it shows how sensitive public companies are to public opinion and to news well beyond their control. It's fraud and a briefcase full of SEC stock market violations. But it shows how you can affect the outcome when you know what the future holds. When the law firms on Wall Street were hacked, the innocuous information stolen was used to trade stocks. The SEC and FBI fumed over the fact that the markets were so easily manipulated. This is the essence of black-and-white crime.

But what happens when the crime is much subtler but just as effective? What happens when social media outlets are used to distribute tuned news stories to "nudge" (just a beat of the butterfly's wing) a business's performance in order to predict stock value and trade accordingly? It's not that unrealistic, since that's what happened in the political furor around Facebook and Cambridge Analytica.[8]

What would happen if stories and ads about a company's products were displayed to social media users? And slowly, the stories caused a drift in thinking? A drift so big that it takes wings on the headwinds of social opinion? Voilà, the company's stock goes up, or like the fictitious Ice Juice story, it goes down. Either way, knowing the outcome means you can buy stock when it's low (knowing the price will go up) or you can "short" the stock, meaning sell stocks you don't own yet with the expectation of being able to buy them at a lower price afterwards. Shorting stock is generally quite risky because if the price goes up, you owe more than you made. But when you know the stock will tumble, it's a safe bet and highly profitable strategy.

Possession of private information (such as company performance) for the purposes of trading stock is referred to as insider trading. And it's very illegal. The SEC views this as a cardinal sin.

But is distributing legitimate stories through social media outlets to a target audience a crime? It is not. Consider the potential impact of stories of batteries in cars spontaneously combusting, or self-driving cars killing their drivers. These stories make great headlines—and powerful headwinds against companies like Tesla.

The point here is that cybercrime can involve not only headline-breaking scams, but also the gentle beating of the butterfly's wings to intentionally create a hurricane. Chaos is not merely theory anymore, it's engineered. Like social engineering, we're talking about market engineering. And the SEC is concerned about this kind of market manipulation and has formed a its own cyber unit to combat this and other forms of cyber fraud. Best of luck.

Cybercrime organizations mimic business organizations

Crime run like a business? It makes sense. Even though they are operating in a virtual realm, cybercrime organizations follow the same MBA approaches our business leaders use. They leverage their commodities, they buy rather than build to reduce operational costs, and they increase efficacy and thereby increase revenue and resulting profit through economies of scale.

It's not much different than other organized crime syndicates, and in some cases, the actors are one and the same.

The yakuza are an Edo-era (seventeenth century) organization, originally devised as a legally recognized group of security guards meant to protect those working on the fringes of society during official religious festivals in Japan. Similar in origin to the Italian mafia, the yakuza were created as a means to allow individuals of lower social rank in communities to trade with the general public without being ostracized or pushed out of trading areas by richer and more powerful merchants. The origin of the word "yakuza" comes from the Japanese Oicho-Kabu card game, where the worst hand you can draw is eight (ya), nine (ku), and three (za)—so "yakuza" means "those who have no value for society." Society did not value these alienated members of their community, and so the yakuza didn't value society.

An investigation that took place over a decade ago revealed that the yakuza generated $56 billion in revenues per year, equating to gross revenues of approximately $650,000 per member.[9] But here's the thing: the yakuza operate mainly as a legitimate corporation, and yet still have many activities under the radar of police around the world. This kind of random relationship between criminal groups and their activities is becoming more prevalent on an international basis, especially as global economic systems become more complex and revenue structures break down. In this context, the deeper the secrecy and more illicit the crime, the easier it is for it to go unnoticed.

And the more society breaks down, the easier it is for organized crime syndicates, including cybercriminals such as the two Andrews, to be able to make money.

The organized cybercrime community is doing just that. They, like other organizations, have partnerships, code-sharing, and service marketplaces. In fact, evidence suggests that cybercriminals are increasingly adopting secure, encrypted consumer applications for private communications to make it harder for outsiders to follow their activity. As well, in the same way as many companies have already migrated data and services to the cloud because of convenience and cost benefits, threat actors are beginning to do so for the same reasons. We've recently observed Azure- and Google-based websites, which anybody can own and to which anyone can upload content, used to host phishing lures and kits. Because these malicious websites use reputable hosts, domain- and IP-based filtering solutions must leave these hosts accessible so businesses can access their data and services. Even worse, there is a tendency for humans and automated detection systems to implicitly trust them and to overlook their associated traffic, leading us down the garden path.

Through our history, we have faced all manner and facets of crime. Back in the 1980s, white-collar crime was an epidemic. Suddenly, we were aware that nonviolent crime was not victimless, and was costlier than its kinetic cousin, bank robbing. As the years wore on, we called embezzling and other forms of similar crime simply that: *crime*. It wasn't white collar or blue collar. It was just crime. And the same will happen with cybercrime. If these trends continue, we will eventually see widespread social structures that help participating threat groups specialize their skill sets in a way that complements the whole cybercrime community. The cybercrime market will become increasingly economically efficient, and very few of us will be able to stop them.

Yes, nation-states no longer discriminate between combatant and civilian. Yes, organized crime is growing in power, but that doesn't mean we should throw our hands up, put our cash under our mattress, and pull the battery from our smartphone. Like any other technology, be it fire, metal tools, or the automobile, there is risk. And we learn to live with the risk because we feel the benefits outweigh the downside.

It's about breaking the cycle and learning from our mistakes so that we stop repeating them. And we can do this if we start thinking differently about the real factors that result in cybercrime, not the ones that we assume matter. In the next chapter, we'll talk about what it really means to work in a world that can never be risk-free, and what we can do to reasonably manage our relationship with risk.

11

THE NEED FOR CHANGE

THE WEATHER WAS unusually warm in late 2019, as Li Wei prepared his stall at the well-known district seafood market. A misnomer, the market housed a thousand nondescript stalls, where local mongers peddled fish, poultry, wild animals like deer, but also meats from animals that brought in a lot of extra money under the table. Li Wei was a humble man in his fifties with a humble business. Most of his money came from the game he could catch and bring to the market, but he knew selling viper meat and bats meant he could make more money to feed his family, and his cousin seemed to enjoy catching these creatures. Besides, snake soup was a popular Cantonese dish. His last customer, a popular chef with a local restaurant, told him diners would pay up to 700 yuan for a cup. He coiled the beheaded reptile and packaged it for his customer, then returned to his chores. As he organized his stall, another customer asked about the pheasant he had on display. After some cajoling, Li Wei nudged his prospective customer through his uncertainty and convinced him that one-pot pheasant was a simple way to honor his girlfriend's mother and show humility while demonstrating his cooking skills.

They exchanged payment, and Li Wei placed the bird in a plastic shopping bag and passed the open handles to his customer, Wang He, who took his purchase and continued his way through the crowded market.

Wang He was excited at the prospect of the meal he would prepare that night. He had secured a good job in a shipping organization through a contact he made during his military service. As he made his way through the market towards the exit, his focus was on his phone as he sent a text to his girlfriend to confirm that his dinner menu was appropriate. That's when he walked right into a smiling old lady at a neighboring counter.

Yu Yan, in her later age, enjoyed trips to the market, and took pride in her weekly show of independence. But today was special. She stood in front of a stall that sold imported flowers. Tonight, she was cooking a farewell meal for her granddaughter, who was visiting from her adopted home in Canada. She poked at the upward-smiling lilies and considered a lucky color to choose for a traveler. Sometimes she struggled reading the fine print, but her granddaughter had taught her a trick: She could use the magnifier function on her smartphone to take a picture and zoom to read the prices. As she lined up to take a picture, something jolted her arm, and before she could react, her phone dropped to the market floor.

Wang He, distracted, had walked into her, hitting her with enough force to knock her phone from her hand. He was ashamed by his inattention and worried he broke her phone. She seemed confused and hesitated to stoop to retrieve the phone he had knocked from her grip. Desperate to make amends, he quickly retrieved the phone and handed it to the old lady. With a red face and embarrassed tone, he quickly shuffled away.

Yu Yan was resilient. And her infectious smile blossomed on her face as she thought about how these young folks walking around with their "smart" phones attached to their noses made their generation anything but smart. As she left the market, the open air brought a gust of wind, blowing dust into her face. She rubbed her eyes to clear the irritant and then headed for the bus home.

Later that night, Jennifer Chang, her granddaughter, helped her prepare a lovely meal and shared stories of sightseeing at the Zhongshan Park. Three days later, Jennifer, an Anglo name that her grandmother detested (she preferred to call her Silly Melon in relation to a childhood incident), said her teary goodbyes and started the long journey back to Canada for Christmas with her friends at university.

A few days later Yu Yan thought her fatigue was a hangover from all the excitement with her granddaughter. But as the flu took hold, it was hard to deny that she was falling ill. Unfightable fatigue, headache, sore throat, and a dry cough signaled the assault that would in a few days lead to her death. Her last thoughts as they turned her onto her stomach in the hospital bed were that doctors relying on modern medicine had lost the way: turning an elderly patient onto her stomach was more barbaric than any traditional remedy. What she didn't realize was that turning was a last-ditch effort to help her fluid-filled lungs expand via gravity and capture the oxygen vital to her survival. With thoughts of her granddaughter, she passed.

Having carried the infection after fixing a problem with her grandmother's phone, Jennifer Chang was infected with the same virus that was going to kill her grandmother. And without symptoms, she was an invisible distribution mechanism, accelerated by handing luggage and boarding passes to airline staff, buying coffee with cash, and touching door handles. Any surface she touched brought contagion to the next people touching it.

This story is fictitious. The people in it aren't real, and the events didn't happen exactly as described. But the virus outbreak is real. The infection was tracked back to the Huanan

Seafood Wholesale Market in the Jianghan District, Wuhan, Hubei province, China. Later, as the related influenza outbreak took a hold in China, it was given a name: Wuhan Coronavirus (COVID-19). An infection-carrying snake or bat was the suspect at the epicenter of the outbreak that would continue to spread around the globe, and at the time of writing, had infected more than 2.5 million people, killed nearly two hundred thousand, and the numbers were rising.‡ Testing had shown that numerous species sold at the market were infected with COVID-19.[1] And, as we know all too well now, the person-to-person spread could occur before an infected individual showed signs or symptoms.

In cybersecurity, original nomenclature derived its terminology from the study of biological infections. We refer to certain attacks as viruses and worms. We compare the way digital viruses spread. But the lessons we can learn from COVID-19 go much deeper than names.

What you don't know can harm you

When we are unaware of a risk or threat, we generally don't take any precautions. Consider the spread of the virus in the story: a food monger handles infected meat; the infection is transferred from his hands to the handles of a plastic carrier bag then touched by his customer. That person then picks up the phone of an elderly lady, further spreading the contamination. She passes it to her granddaughter, who then exposes hundreds of people to the virus less than a week later.

This all happens long before anyone shows signs of the disease.

---

‡   At the time of writing, the cross-species transmission of COVID-19 was attributed to snakes and bats.

In cybersecurity, often the threat lurks in the wild without our prior knowledge. The day we do eventually discover it is not day three, day two, or even day one: this is day zero. It's day zero because it's the first time we've seen it, and as with a coronavirus, we need time to model the virus and develop a vaccination. Just as humans had no developed antibody to the novel coronavirus, most antivirus systems can't stop what they can't recognize as malicious.

Ignorance is not bliss, it's negligence

Data breaches, lawsuits, insurance claims, and so on converge to create a line in the sand when it comes to expectation and accountability. We must assume we are under attack, and we must understand the obligations associated with the nature of our business, and the data we manage. What's more, we must be consistent in our approach. Once we identify a risk, there is no plausible denial. We are obligated to manage this risk.

Consider all the basic efforts medical organizations recommend: cover your cough, wash your hands regularly, avoid sick people, stay away from public areas. Even if we could adhere to all these recommendations, the virus still spreads. Some viruses spread rapidly and can disrupt as much through their threat—causing drastic but necessary preventive measures—as through their direct effects. As well, like the spread of a mutating virus, cyberattacks mutate, something called polymorphism. They work to avoid detection. And they can't be stopped with simple check-box approaches. Basic hygiene is necessary but not sufficient.

Most companies have antivirus software and firewalls; similar forms of hygiene involve avoiding visiting questionable websites (like unlicensed media streaming sites), using strong passwords, and training your employees so they know about the threats. As we've seen in this book, all the companies that were attacked did these things. It's hygiene, not inoculation. These precautions are necessary and play a role in eliminating what I call the background radiation of the internet. They protect your business from nuisance malware and wasted cycles cleaning computer systems, resetting passwords, and sending alert emails to your employees. But it's backward looking, and akin to attempting to predict who will commit a crime by data mining arrest records. It can only predict future acts by known offenders. These practices won't stop attacks that don't use malware. They won't stop attacks that use your trusted systems against you. They won't stop the "hands-on-keyboard" attacks launched by organized criminals and nation-states.

Security is an elixir of people, processes, and technology. It takes good guys to combat bad guys. And the expertise needs will adapt and morph over time. There is no single solution. There is no "easy" button.

Criminals will kick you when you are down

The threats don't wait in line to come one at a time, either. If a threat or attack from one side weakens or distracts you, an attacker from another side will want to use that to their advantage. Coronavirus-related cyberattacks have taken advantage of fear and confusion: Over four thousand websites related to COVID-19 were registered between January and March of 2020, including a significant contingent of malicious sites, some of which lured visitors using fraudulent hot-zone maps.[2] Other phishing attacks used PDF and Microsoft Word health care documents to deploy remote access tools and clipboard copying, keystroke logging, desktop image capture, and a cornucopia of malware.[3]

In the 2011 Hollywood thriller *Contagion*, a form of bat flu called MEV-1 ravages the world after emerging from an unknown source in Hong Kong and spreading to the American Midwest by a returning business traveler.[4] The movie foretold the social, political, and economic impacts of a global pandemic. Even more accurately, it illustrated how people or organizations take advantage of these situations for their own gain, including spreading misinformation for profit, as seen by Jude Law's character, touting a naturopathic cure called Forsythia. With COVID-19, a plethora of scams evolved, including text messages for free iPhones[5] and free Android malware that accesses cameras and microphones to snoop.[6] Even text messages from the supposedly infected, pleading for help, emerged.[7]

Jude Law's conspiracy theorist character, Alan Krumwiede, claims online that he was cured of MEV-1 by homeopathic Forsythia (later to be proven false). His social followers overwhelm pharmacies and riot in search of the supplement. And like Forsythia, unapproved and questionable cures and treatments for COVID-19 sprang up: Silver Sol liquid, gels and lozenges touted by 1980s televangelist Jim Bakker;[8] Coronavirus Boneset Tea and tinctures;[9] and toothpaste and dietary supplements promoted by *InfoWars* radio host Alex Jones.[10] Warning letters and cease-and-desist notices did little to slow the crop of coronavirus weeds. Amazon removed over one million products that claimed to treat COVID-19 and removed tens of thousands of deals from merchants that Amazon said attempted to price-gouge customers.[11] Worse, police authorities around the globe issued warnings about door-to-door culprits, posing as Red Cross or medical examiner officials attempting to scam unwitting victims in their homes![12]

It seems *Contagion* got it right: "Nothing spreads like fear."

This is nothing new. It's a well-rehearsed playbook, exploiting the same chaos and fear as is caused by major weather or other natural disasters. Similar attacks occurred back in 2012 and early 2013 during and after the chaos caused in New York by Hurricane Sandy. During the weeks around the debilitating storm, traffic across law and financial firms dropped by up to 30 percent, while malware and other malicious traffic increased by the same number. And without power, and with flooded subway lines preventing employees from getting to Manhattan offices, those firms were left exposed to cyberattacks.

What works today won't work tomorrow

Like the virus at the heart of the coronavirus story, malware and cyberattacks morph over time. In terms of malware, polymorphic adaption can help viruses to evade simplistic antivirus and firewall defenses. And criminal techniques adapt over time, ever more finely honed by the lessons that they have learned from previous successful and unsuccessful attacks. Criminals are now so good at mimicking trusted and legitimate sources that you can no longer trust anyone or anything. In the business of cybersecurity, this environment is actually called "zero trust."

In industry terms, we are facing an ever-evolving threat landscape. Companies now feel the cyber aftershocks of political decisions like trade wars or missile exchanges. Nation-states or state-sponsored groups no longer delineate between combatants and civilians. There is no collateral damage, just damage. Organized criminal organizations apply Fortune 500 business principles to streamline their operations and grow their revenue. They employ best-in-class technology and techniques, and often use your own tools against you.

And we willingly inflict risk-bringing change upon ourselves.

The one constant in our interconnected world is change. The ubiquitous digitization of every aspect of business drives an ever-increasing adoption of emerging technology. Digital transformation is dominated by nebulous perimeters, distributed workforces, global connections, artificial intelligence–driven decision-making and critical systems moving to the public cloud. It creates a never-ending flow of new features, approaches, and business models. Although invigorating, this self-feeding tech frenzy creates a petri dish ideal for the growth of misuse and abuse of these emerging technologies and new processes. Rapid change sometimes limits understanding and introduces risk into the ecosystem. Yet this "leap before looking" approach dominates when business requirements force adoption as a means of survival.

It's time to change our approach to security

Washing your hands and covering your mouth when you cough helps, but as with COVID-19 (and similar viruses like SARS-CoV or MERS-CoV), prevention only goes so far.

The same is true in cybersecurity. Traditional approaches have focused on prevention. There is an assumption that if we lock our windows and doors, we won't be broken into. Well, locks keep good people out, but it turns out that criminals don't follow rules, and don't mind breaking locks, windows, and double-walled doors in order to enter. For decades, we've labored with notions of building higher, unclimbable walls just to see criminals simply go around them. We spend billions on prevention security only to see trillions lost to cybercrime.

We need to shift our focus in two dimensions.

The first is to rely on prevention technology to find the known, while we use a mix of technology and security experts to find the unknown. This model is based on the idea of predictive or proactive security. It's about enabling your organization to quickly identify and investigate threats and then take action to contain or disrupt detected attacks. It's the cleaning up of spilled milk to avoid the business-disrupting results of metastasized cyberattacks.

But that's the technical paradigm shift. That's the easier one.

The harder shift, the second dimension, moves security from the domain of IT to that of the boardroom. As I've taught throughout this book, cybersecurity is not an IT problem to solve, it's a business risk to manage.

We can start to build a new mindset around protecting our businesses and our sense of security by being prepared for the right risks, right now.

But before we do that, we have to recognize our limitations. Everything we own is now "smart." First our phones, then our watches, our TVs, our door locks, and so on. Our cities are on the cusp of being smart. With the next generation of mobile service providers, called 5G, almost every device we have will be constantly connected. We won't just be swimming in a Wi-Fi pool at home and running down the street to a coffee shop to find the next pool of low-cost internet connection; we will be in an ocean of data wherever we go. With 5G, Ericsson predicts that almost half of the data in the world will transit mobile networks.[13] This essentially means all of us, via our devices, will be constantly connected. The problem won't be worrying about finding a connection. It will become the opposite. How do I switch off? How do I disconnect?

Think of printed books. They brought knowledge to the masses. Now we often read digital versions on digital devices that require internet access to verify digital rights, and power to literally keep the light on. Physical books have no requirements (other than basic literacy) and don't measure their time to read with a battery meter. So, what happens when you can't access the book? Or the book is no longer the accurate and author-intended material but some hijacked version of its original narrative?

We've come to depend on ubiquitous power sources and connectivity. But when our devices are always on, we're supposed to be always on ourselves. And by extension, always vigilant. And I'm not sure we quite ready for that yet.

As we've seen and read about here, we aggressively adopt new technology and then reactively address security issues. We see the security challenges in IoT-connected devices in medical facilities, and smart assembly lines in manufacturing plants. What happens when our cities are smart, and our opt-out choices become slim to none? Criminals are smart also. They will find ways of exploiting our desire for omnipresence and omniscience. There will be nowhere to hide, and your business will always be vulnerable to attacks. Talk about weapons of mass destruction! Municipalities themselves have fallen prey to cybercriminals—are they prepared for the onslaught over their smart grids? And the mobile or wireless service providers we rely on to travel their 5G highway will now become the guardians of the kingdom. Are they prepared to change and invest as necessary to prevent pan-prey behaviors or mass umbrella attacks and outages?

But we also know that, over the past few years, the social and economic impact of cybercrime has garnered more attention from law enforcement and politicians, and things are slowly shifting towards prioritizing cybersecurity, and making that smart as well. Attacks are no longer a nuisance or mild inconvenience; there is growing recognition that they are reaching a pandemic or crisis stage, with headline-grabbing service outages at hospitals, shutdowns of government services, billions of dollars lost to ransoms and downtime, and concerns about industrial espionage against a backdrop of numerous global trade disputes. That's why, in 2015,

President Barack Obama issued an executive order that empowered the treasury secretary to block the financial assets of individuals that use cyber weapons to harm American companies and citizens, an effort that has not been overturned by the current administration—for good reason.

A few factors contribute to why these changes are on the horizon. First, law enforcement and cybersecurity agencies are receiving larger budgets for investigations of cybersecurity incidents. Second, the skills and experience within these agencies has increased significantly, with many investing in training from outside experts. And third, some threat actors are switching sides, whether out of a change of heart or to earn leniency in the justice system.

So, if the rules are changing, what can small- and medium-sized businesses do to also move towards a safer future? To be really, truly smart about it? As I mentioned at the beginning of this book, all the breaches I've witnessed have the same contributing factors. Each victim company was repeating the same cycle of false assumptions about their lack of value to criminals, and a check-box mentality towards cybersecurity. All of them set aside the opportunity to strategize their risk management in favor of placing the burden on technological solutions with few, if any, ongoing assessments. We repeat the same mistakes over and over. Often, when you see a pattern repeating it's a sign that you are stuck in a cycle. It's a lesson you've failed to learn. Or a truth to accept.

A commitment to smart cybersecurity is an opportunity to make a different set of choices than we have in the past.

Companies, no matter the industry, need to find a compromise between IT practices and the market pressures that influence business decisions. Our security programs must align with our business objectives. All parties, C-suite through all levels of employees and their supply chain stakeholders, as well as technical practitioners, must harmonize their activities with the primary goal of protecting their business from cyber attackers. We need to understand why everyone on the team makes the decisions they do. And we want to seek forward accountability, rather than look back to the past.

Risks aren't going to be eliminated, even when we plan ahead. We know this. But with all that we know, we can still manage our relationship with risk. Revisiting and constantly reminding ourselves of the core pillars of cyber protection is a good place to start:

- **AWARENESS:** What do you need to know right now about cyber risks and trends? How can you continue to arm yourself with the best knowledge out there, and how can you ensure that your organizational team knows what they need to know? Who's updating the executive team, and when?

- **RISK:** How are you continuously identifying and tracking your nonpublic assets and protected data, and documenting regulatory and contractual obligations?

- **PROGRAM:** Are your budget, staffing, and programs for your risk priorities established? Are they enough? Are you covered for eventualities that insurance won't cover?

- **REPORTING:** Is your annual planning, quarterly reporting, and assessment protocol up to standard? Is it reaching the level of your peers, industry expectations, and customer assumptions?

- **INCIDENTS:** What's your plan of action for incident response? Are your board roles, critical business decisions, crisis communications, and other protocols locked down? Have you practiced the plan? Have you subjected it to a gap analysis or risk audit?

It's important that, like the criminal adversaries out there, we build better ways of sharing what we know and what we can do, and collectively learn from our mistakes.

We are more connected than ever. We have millennia of knowledge at our fingertips. And, more than ever, we can access this information by conjuring answers through our digital assistants. We have to learn, however, how to sit down with each other and ensure that things change. The biggest barrier is the language we use to talk about cybersecurity in our organizations, and finding the Rosetta stone that translates ones and zeros to dollar signs and reputation. We have to be transparent about what really matters when it comes to risk, and ensure that those with knowledge have a seat at the table, and an open door to discuss those risks without censure.

But we can do this.

As the Buddha is often quoted as saying, "Thousands of candles can be lit from a single candle." Early Chinese images of the Buddha, in the guise of the bodhisattva of infinite compassion and mercy, Guanyin, often depict him as sitting in a state of calm, being surrounded by beasts and dragons, to illustrate the deity's power to save all people from perils. When we shine the light in the dark, and when we pass that light to each other through shared knowledge and support, we can do just the same.

NOTES

Introduction

1. Wikipedia, s.v., "Sutton's Law," updated November 17, 2018, https://en
.wikipedia.org/wiki/Sutton%27s_law.
2. Christine Marciano, "Cyber Insurance Claim Study Shows SMEs Are
Getting Hit the Hardest with Cyber Incidents," Data Breach Insurance, October 10, 2019, https://databreachinsurancequote.com/cyber
-insurance/cyber-insurance-claims-study-shows-smbs-are-getting-hit
-the-hardest-with-cyber-incidents/.
3. Wikipedia, s.v., "Sutton's Law."

1: Chaos Reigns

1. Michael Kan, "Smart Teddy Bears Involved in a Contentious Data Breach,"
NetworkWorld, February 27, 2017, https://www.networkworld.com/article/
3175225/smart-teddy-bears-involved-in-a-contentious-data-breach.html.
2 . Michael Cukier, "Study: Hackers Attack Every 39 Seconds," A. James
Clark School of Engineering, February 9, 2007, https://eng.umd.edu/
news/story/study-hackers-attack-every-39-seconds.
3. "2019 On Track to Being the 'Worst Year on Record' for Breach Activity," Risk Based Security, accessed April 13, 2020, https://pages.riskbased
security.com/2019-midyear-data-breach-quickview-report.
4. "IC3 Annual Report Released," FBI, April 22, 2019, https://www.fbi.gov/
news/stories/ic3-releases-2018-internet-crime-report-042219.

5. Rahul Vyas, "The Ascendant Cycle of Cyber Crimes: An Ordeal for the Present Legal Framework," *Pacific University Journal of Social Sciences* 1, no. 2 (May 25, 2017), https://ssrn.com/abstract=3035826.

6. *The Secret Life of Chaos: Chaos Theory*, with Jim Al-Khalili, directed and produced by Nic Stacey, January 14, 2010, video, 59:58, https://www.you tube.com/watch?v=p_yOueFMe7c.

7. Wikipedia, s.v., "Red Queen Hypothesis," updated April 13, 2020, https:// en.wikipedia.org/wiki/Red_Queen_hypothesis.

8. Steve Morgan, "Cybercrime Damages $6 Trillion by 2021," *Cybercrime Magazine*, October 16, 2017, https://cybersecurityventures.com/hacker pocalypse-cybercrime-report-2016/.

9. Martin Evans, "Computer Hacker Who Blackmailed Porn Users Jailed after UK's 'Most Serious' Cyber Crime Investigation," *Telegraph*, April 9, 2019, https://www.telegraph.co.uk/news/2019/04/09/computer-hacker -blackmailed-porn-users-jailed-uks-serious-cyber/.

10. J. Watkins, "No Good Deed Goes Unpunished: The Duties Held by Malware Researchers, Penetration Testers, and 'White Hat' Hackers," *Minnesota Journal of Law, Science & Technology* 19, no. 2 (2018): 535, https://scholarship.law.umn.edu/mjlst/vol19/iss2/7.

11. "Norsk Hydro Cyber Attack Cost It Nearly $52M in First Quarter," *Insurance Journal*, April 30, 2019, https://www.insurancejournal.com/news/ international/2019/04/30/525093.htm.

12. "Panama Papers Law Firm Mossack Fonseca to Shut Down after Tax Scandal," Reuters, March 14, 2018, https://www.reuters.com/article/us-panama -corruption/panama-papers-law-firm-mossack-fonseca-to-shut-down -after-tax-scandal-idUSKCN1GQ34R.

13. M. Singh, J.A. Husain, and N.K. Vishwas, "A Comprehensive Study of Cyber Law and Cyber Crimes," *International Journal of IT, Engineering and Applied Sciences Research (IJIEASR)* 3, no. 2 (2014): 20–24, http://citeseerx .ist.psu.edu/viewdoc/download?doi=10.1.1.428.4679&rep=rep1&type=pdf.

14. J. Kosseff, "Defining Cybersecurity Law," *Iowa Law Review* 103, no. 3 (2017): 985, https://ilr.law.uiowa.edu/print/volume-103-issue-3/defining -cybersecurity-law/.

2: No More Ones and Zeros

1. Joe Morgenstern, "The Fifty-Nine-Story Crisis," *The New Yorker*, May 29, 1995, 45–53, https://www.lemessurier.com/sites/default/files/publications/ _59-StoryCrisis%20Neworker%20May1995.pdf.

2. "Wireless Tower Operator Sues Chief of Rival," *New York Times*, December 29, 2007, https://www.nytimes.com/2007/12/29/technology/29lawsuit .html.

3.   Josh Rogin, "Exclusive: Controversial Obama U.N. Nominee Withdraws for 'Personal Reasons,' Official Says," *Foreign Policy*, December 29, 2009, https://foreignpolicy.com/2009/12/29/exclusive-controversial-obama -u-n-nominee-withdraws-for-personal-reasons-official-says/.

4.   "Ponemon Study: Only 28 Percent of Enterprises Say CEO and Board Approves Acceptable Level of Cyber Risk, Demonstrating Clear Lack of Accountability," Business Wire, October 15, 2019, https://www.business wire.com/news/home/20191015005326/en/Ponemon-Study-28-Percent -Enterprises-CEO-Board.

5.   "NACD Director's Handbook on Cyber-Risk Oversight," NACD, February 25, 2020, https://www.nacdonline.org/insights/publications.cfm?Item Number=67298.

6.   "Board Toolkit," National Cyber Security Centre, March 21, 2019, https:// www.ncsc.gov.uk/collection/board-toolkit.

7.   Matt Aiello, Philipp Amann, Mark Anderson, et al., *Navigating the Digital Age: The Definitive Cybersecurity Guide for Directors and Officers*, 2nd ed. (Palo Alto: Palo Alto Networks, Inc., 2015), https://www.securityroundtable .org/navigating-the-digital-age-2nd-edition/.

3: You're Going to Need a Bigger Boat

1.   "Business Email Compromise the $26 Billion Scam," FBI, September 10, 2019, https://www.ic3.gov/media/2019/190910.aspx.

2.   Mia Galuppo, "'You're Gonna Need a Bigger Boat': 'Jaws' Writer Reveals Origins of Movie's Famous Line," *Hollywood Reporter*, March 7, 2016, https://www.hollywoodreporter.com/news/jaws-bigger-boat-quote-writer -872226.

3.   "Formal Opinion 483: Lawyers' Obligations after an Electronic Data Breach or Cyberattack," American Bar Association, October 17, 2018, https:// www.americanbar.org/content/dam/aba/administrative/professional_ responsibility/aba_formal_op_483.pdf.

4: Only from Disaster Can We Be Resurrected

1.   Sidney Dekker, *The Field Guide to Understanding 'Human Error'*, 3rd ed. (Boca Raton: CRC Press, 2014).

2.   *Federal Trade Commission v. Equifax Inc.*, 2361, United States District Court, July 22, 2019, https://www.ftc.gov/system/files/documents/cases/ 172_3203_equifax_complaint_7-22-19.pdf.

3.   Richard Feynman, "Los Alamos from Below: Reminiscences," Caltech, accessed April 14, 2020, http://calteches.library.caltech.edu/34/3/Feyn manLosAlamos.htm.

4.   "Third-Party Risk to the Nth Degree," eSentire, June 20, 2019, https://www.esentire.com/resource-library/third-party-risk-to-the-nth-degree/.

5.   "23 NYCRR 500: Cybersecurity Requirements for Financial Services Companies," New York State Department of Financial Services, March 1, 2017, 7–8, https://www.dfs.ny.gov/docs/legal/regulations/adoptions/dfsrf500txt.pdf.

5: No Safe Spaces

1.   Rowland Manthorpe, "Coronavirus: Cybercriminals Target Healthcare Workers with Email Scam," Sky News, March 13, 2020, https://news.sky.com/story/coronavirus-cybercriminals-target-healthcare-workers-with-email-scam-11956617.

2.   Alex Scroxton, "Coronavirus-Linked Hacks Likely as Czech Hospital Comes Under Attack," Computer Weekly, March 13, 2020, https://www.computerweekly.com/news/252480022/Coronavirus-linked-hacks-likely-as-Czech-hospital-comes-under-attack.

3.   S.J. Choi, M.E. Johnson, and C.U. Lehmann, "Data Breach Remediation Efforts and Their Implications for Hospital Quality," *Health Services Research* 54, no. 5 (2019): 971–80, https://doi.org/10.1111/1475-6773.13203.

4.   William Alexander, "Barnaby Jack Could Hack Your Pacemaker and Make Your Heart Explode," *Vice*, June 25, 2013, https://www.vice.com/en_ca/article/avnx5j/i-worked-out-how-to-remotely-weaponise-a-pacemaker.

5.   "Key Findings of the 2019 Verizon Data Breach Investigations Report," *HIPAA Journal*, May 8, 2019, https://www.hipaajournal.com/2019-verizon-data-breach-investigations-report-findings/.

6.   Nicole Wetsman, "Health Care's Huge Cybersecurity Problem," *The Verge*, April 4, 2019, https://www.theverge.com/2019/4/4/18293817/cybersecurity-hospitals-health-care-scan-simulation.

6: All the Plans in the World

1.   Joseph Cox, "Hackers Claim Theft of Data from Gorilla Glue," *Vice*, Motherboard, November 17, 2016, https://www.vice.com/en_us/article/53dq8k/hackers-claim-theft-of-data-from-gorilla-glue.

2.   Joseph Cox, "'Dark Overlord' Hackers Text Death Threats to Students, Then Dump Voicemails from Students," *The Daily Beast*, October 5, 2017, https://www.thedailybeast.com/dark-overlord-hackers-text-death-threats-to-students-then-dump-voicemails-from-victims.

3.   Harlan Coben, *The Stranger* (London: Orion Books, 2015).

4. Justin Rohrlich, "A Massive International Email Scam Netted $3 Million Worth of Top-Secret US Military Equipment," *Quartz*, July 9, 2019, https:// qz.com/1661537/us-defense-contractor-falls-for-3-million-email-scam/.

7: The Domino Effect

1. "The Deepwater Horizon," *Seconds from Disaster*, season 5, episode 5, directed by Stan Griffin, National Geographic documentary, aired April 15, 2012.
2. "The Deepwater Horizon."
3. "Third-Party Risk to the Nth Degree," eSentire, June 20, 2019, https:// www.esentire.com/resource-library/third-party-risk-to-the-nth-degree/.
4. "23 NYCRR 500: Cybersecurity Requirements for Financial Services Companies," New York State Department of Financial Services, March 1, 2017, 7–8, https://www.dfs.ny.gov/docs/legal/regulations/adoptions/ dfsrf500txt.pdf.
5. "Supply Chain Security Guidance," National Cyber Security Centre, January 28, 2018, https://www.ncsc.gov.uk/collection/supply-chain-security.

8: Gray Crime and Punishment

1. "Dark Web Paedophile Matthew Falder Blackmailed Victims," BBC News, February 7, 2018, https://www.bbc.com/news/uk-england-birmingham -42975202.
2. Capstone IT, "Cybercrime Is Bigger Than the Drug Trade: Why Small- and Medium-Sized Businesses Are More Susceptible to Online Threats," *Buffalo Business First*, June 5, 2019, https://www.bizjournals.com/buffalo/ news/2019/06/05/cybercrime-is-bigger-than-the-drug-trade-why-small .html.
3. *2010 Internet Crime Report*, National White Collar Crime Center, 2011, https://pdf.ic3.gov/2010_IC3Report.pdf.
4. *Criminal Resource Manual*, U.S. Department of Justice, 2019, http://www .justice.gov/usam/criminal-resource-manual.
5. Bethania Palma, "No, Red Cross Is Not Offering Coronavirus Home Tests," Snopes, updated March 19, 2020, https://www.snopes.com/fact-check/ red-cross-coronavirus-scams/.
6. "Software Management: Security Imperative, Business Opportunity," BSA Global Software Survey, June 2018, https://gss.bsa.org/wp-content/ uploads/2018/05/2018_BSA_GSS_Report_en.pdf.
7. "Report to the Nations: 2020 Global Study on Occupational Fraud and Abuse," Association of Certified Fraud Examiners, https://acfepublic.s3 -us-west-2.amazonaws.com/2020-Report-to-the-Nations.pdf.

8. Peter Driscoll, "Remarks at the SIFMA Operations Conference & Exhibition: Staying Vigilant to Protect Investors," U.S. Securities and Exchange Commission, May 8, 2019, https://www.sec.gov/news/speech/driscoll-remarks-sifma-operations-conference-050819.

9. Max Daly, "Inside the Repulsive World of 'Hurtcore,' the Worst Crimes Imaginable," *Vice*, February 19, 2018, https://www.vice.com/en_uk/article/59kye3/the-repulsive-world-of-hurtcore-the-worst-crimes-imaginable.

9: No One Has Your Back

1. Daniel Woods and Tyler Moore, "Does Insurance Have a Future in Governing Cybersecurity?" *IEEE Security & Privacy* 18, no. 1 (January/February 2020): 21–27, https://doi.org/10.1109/MSEC.2019.2935702.

2. "Managing the Risks in Cyberspace," American Academy of Actuaries, accessed April 14, 2020, https://www.actuary.org/content/managing-risks-cyberspace.

3. *The Plane That Fell from the Sky* (documentary), CBS News, produced by Paul Fine and Holly Fine, aired July 14, 1983, 50:43.

4. H.G. Bissinger, "11 Years after Plane Took a Dive, Pilot Tries to Clear His Reputation," *Chicago Tribune*, October 14, 1990, https://www.chicagotribune.com/news/ct-xpm-1990-10-14-9003260194-story.html.

5. Bissinger, "11 Years after Plane Took a Dive."

6. Benjamin Franklin, "It takes many good deeds…" BrainyQuote, accessed April 14, 2020, https://www.brainyquote.com/quotes/benjamin_franklin_385547.

7. Nicola Slawson, "Mossack Fonseca Law Firm to Shut Down after Panama Papers Tax Scandal," *Guardian*, March 14, 2018, https://www.theguardian.com/world/2018/mar/14/mossack-fonseca-shut-down-panama-papers.

8. Tristan Jonckheer, "Cyber Insurance: What Is It Good For?" Dentons, October 16, 2019, https://www.dentons.com/en/insights/alerts/2019/october/16/cyber-insurance-what-is-it-good-for.

9. "Avoiding the Most Common Cyber Insurance Claim Denials," GB&A, accessed April 14, 2020, https://www.gbainsurance.com/avoiding-cyber-claim-denials.

10. Alex Hern, "Fitness Tracking App Strava Gives Away Location of Secret US Army Bases," *Guardian*, January 20, 2018, https://www.theguardian.com/world/2018/jan/28/fitness-tracking-app-gives-away-location-of-secret-us-army-bases.

10: The Next War

1. "Charlottesville and Beyond," Anti-Defamation League, accessed April 14, 2020, https://www.adl.org/education/resources/tools-and-strategies/table-talk/charlottesville-and-beyond.

2. J. Hell and G. Steinmetz, "A Period of 'Wild and Fierce Fanaticism': Populism, Theo-political Militarism, and the Crisis of US Hegemony," *American Journal of Cultural Sociology* 5, no. 3 (2017): 373–91, https://doi.org/10.1057/s41290-017-0041-y.

3. Luke O'Brien, "The Making of an American Nazi," *The Atlantic*, December 2017, https://www.theatlantic.com/magazine/archive/2017/12/the-making-of-an-american-nazi/544119/.

4. "About Andrew Anglin," Southern Poverty Law Center, accessed April 14, 2020, https://www.splcenter.org/fighting-hate/extremist-files/individual/andrew-anglin.

5. "About Andrew Anglin."

6. Adi Roberston, "Neo-Nazi Site Moves to Dark Web after GoDaddy and Google Bans," *The Verge*, August 15, 2017, https://www.theverge.com/2017/8/15/16150668/daily-stormer-alt-right-dark-web-site-godaddy-google-ban.

7. Aruna Vishwanatha, Dustin Volz, and Kate O'Keeffe, "Four Members of China's Military Indicted Over Massive Equifax Breach," *Wall Street Journal*, updated February 11, 2020, https://www.wsj.com/articles/four-members-of-china-s-military-indicted-for-massive-equifax-breach-11581346824.

8. Wikipedia, s.v., "Facebook–Cambridge Analytica Data Scandal," updated April 13, 2020, https://en.wikipedia.org/wiki/Facebook%E2%80%93Cambridge_Analytica_data_scandal.

9. Peter Hill, "Heisei Yakuza: Burst Bubble and *Bôtaihô*," Sociology Working Papers, Paper Number 2002-10, 2003, https://pdfs.semanticscholar.org/ae64/098553af58684e78ce448455501907ee4832.pdf.

11: The Need for Change

1. Jeremy Page, "Virus Sparks Soul-Searching Over China's Wild Animal Trade," *Wall Street Journal*, January 26, 2020, https://www.wsj.com/articles/virus-sparks-soul-searching-over-chinas-wild-animal-trade-11580055290.

2. Anthony Spadafora, "Hackers Are Spreading Malware through Coronavirus Maps," *TechRadar*, March 11, 2020, https://www.techradar.com/news/hackers-are-spreading-malware-through-coronavirus-maps.

3. Elizabeth Montalbano, "Spread of Coronavirus-Themed Cyberattacks Persist with New Attacks," *Threatpost*, March 6, 2020, https://threatpost.com/coronavirus-themed-cyberattacks-persists/153493/.

4. Wikipedia, s.v., "*Contagion* (2011 Film), Plot," updated April 13, 2020, https://en.wikipedia.org/wiki/Contagion_(2011_film)#Plot.

5. Katie Porter (@katieporteroc), "As a consumer protection attorney and consumer advocate I have seen corrupt organizations scam those most vulnerable. During this pandemic, it is important to be diligent and on the lookout …," Twitter, March 16, 2020, https://twitter.com/katieporteroc/status/1239698845354741761?s=20.

6. Thomas Brewster, "Coronavirus Scam Alert: COVID-19 Map Malware Can Spy on You through Your Android Microphone and Camera," *Forbes*, March 18, 2020, https://www.forbes.com/sites/thomasbrewster/2020/03/18/coronavirus-scam-alert-covid-19-map-malware-can-spy-on-you-through-your-android-microphone-and-camera/#4017455375fd.

7. Mark Sangster (@mbsangster), "More examples of #COVID19 scams. Be skeptical. #CyberAttack #NoSafeHarbor," Twitter, March 20, 2020, https://twitter.com/mbsangster/status/1241018548711034880?s=20.

8. Lesley Fair, "FTC, FDA Warn Companies Making Coronavirus Claims," Federal Trade Commission, March 9, 2020, https://www.ftc.gov/news-events/blogs/business-blog/2020/03/ftc-fda-warn-companies-making-coronavirus-claims.

9. William A. Correll and Richard Quaresima, U.S. Food and Drug Administration, warning letter to Amy Weidner, Herbal Amy Inc., subject: "Unapproved and Misbranded Products Related to Coronavirus Disease 2019 (COVID-19)," March 6, 2020, https://www.ftc.gov/system/files/attachments/press-releases/ftc/fda-covid-warning-letters/wl_to_herbal_amy_covid-19_occ_cleared_3-5-20_cleanversion_qttrq2_002.pdf.

10. "Attorney General James Orders Alex Jones to Stop Selling Fake Coronavirus Treatments," Letitia James NY Attorney General, March 12, 2020, https://ag.ny.gov/press-release/2020/attorney-general-james-orders-alex-jones-stop-selling-fake-coronavirus-treatments.

11. Jeffery Dastin, "Amazon Bars One Million Products for False Coronavirus Claims," Reuters, February 27, 2020, https://www.reuters.com/article/us-china-health-amazon-com/amazon-bars-one-million-products-for-false-coronavirus-claims-idUSKCN20L2ZH.

12. Greg David, "Coronavirus: Peterborough Police Warn of COVID-19 Scams," *Global News*, March 17, 2020, https://globalnews.ca/news/6690907/coronavirus-peterborough-scams/; James Wood, "Coronavirus Scams Warning: Fraudsters Are Posing as WHO Officials to Dupe Victims Says

Finance Body—While Police Warn of Gangs Offering Bogus Tests," *Daily Mail*, March 18, 2020, https://www.dailymail.co.uk/news/article-8125383/ Police-issue-warning-coronavirus-scamming-gangs-offering-people -bogus-tests-doorstep.html; Associated Press, "Coronavirus Scam: Police Warn Against False Virus Infection Claims," CBS *Baltimore*, March 18, 2020, https://baltimore.cbslocal.com/2020/03/18/coronavirus-maryland-police -warn-against-false-virus-inspection-claims/; "FBI and Police Warn of Coronavirus Scam, a Trick to Ransom Your Phone or Computer," *ABC4 News*, March 16, 2020, https://www.abc4.com/news/fbi-and-police-warn -of-coronavirus-scam-a-trick-to-ransom-your-phone-or-computer/; Sarah M. Wojcik, "Pennsylvania State Police Warn Public of Coronavirus-Related Scams," *The Morning Call*, March 17, 2020, https://www.mcall.com/corona virus/mc-nws-coronavirus-scam-warning-20200317-ahk2v3jtvjezrnm4m 4xptdoztq-story.html; Kaylyn Hlavaty, "Police Departments across Northeast Ohio Warn of At-Home COVID-19 Testing Scams," *ABC News 5 Cleveland*, March 18, 2020, https://www.news5cleveland.com/news/ continuing-coverage/coronavirus/police-departments-across-northeast -ohio-warn-of-at-home-covid-19-testing-scams.

13. "Building 5G Networks," Ericsson, accessed April 14, 2020, https://www .ericsson.com/en/5g/5g-networks.

INDEX

ABOUT THE AUTHOR

MARK SANGSTER is an award-winning speaker at international conferences and on prestigious stages, including the Harvard Law School, and an author on various subjects related to cybersecurity. He is a contributor to several leading industry publications (*CSO* magazine, *SC* magazine, *Legaltech News*), an invited speaker at numerous conferences, and a regular guest on well-respected podcasts.

His thought-provoking work and perspective on shifting risk trends has influenced industry thought leaders, and he is a go-to subject matter expert on data breach events for top publications and media outlets, including the *Wall Street Journal* and the CBC. Mark has served on the LegalSEC Council with the International Legal Technology Association, and now advises the National Association of Manufacturers on their cybersecurity policies.

His twenty-five-year career was established with industry giants like Intel Corporation, BlackBerry, and Cisco Systems. At BlackBerry, Mark worked on the first secure devices for government agencies. Since then, he has continued to build mutually beneficial relationships with regulatory agencies in key industry sectors, including legal, finance, health care, and manufacturing.